THE LITTLE
BLACK BOOK OF

PARIS

The Essential Guide to the
City of Light

VESNA NESKOW

MAPS BY DAVID LINDROTH, INC.

ILLUSTRATED BY
KERREN BARBAS STECKLER

PETER PAUPER PRESS, INC.
WHITE PLAINS, NEW YORK

FOR TANYA AND PETE,
WHO FIRST GAVE ME THE
GIFT OF TRAVEL

Editor: Mara Conlon
Proofreader: JCommunications, LLC

Designed by Heather Zschock

Illustrations copyright © 2006 Kerren Barbas
Paris Métro Map © 2009 Régie Autonome des Transports
Parisens (RATP). Used with permission.
Neighborhood maps © 2009 David Lindroth Inc.

2nd Edition

Copyright © 2009
Peter Pauper Press, Inc.
202 Mamaroneck Avenue
White Plains, NY 10601
All rights reserved
ISBN 978-1-59359-840-2
Printed in Hong Kong
7 6 5 4 3 2 1

The publisher has made every effort to ensure that the content of this book was current at the time of publication. It's always best, however, to confirm information before making final travel plans, since telephone numbers, Web sites, prices, hours of operation, and other facts are always subject to change. The publisher cannot accept responsibility for any consequences arising from the use of this book. We value your feedback and suggestions. Please write to: Editors, Peter Pauper Press, Inc., 202 Mamaroneck Avenue, Suite 400, White Plains, New York 10601-5376.

Visit us at www.peterpauper.com

THE LITTLE
BLACK BOOK OF
PARIS

CONTENTS

INTRODUCTION

Paris conjures visions of sophistication, drama, and romance. The clichés abound, yet there's no denying the allure and beauty of the City of Light. Flamboyant and mysterious, Gothic and modern, refined and bawdy—Paris is all these, with room for both grandeur and coziness. It is a city imbued with history, a center of art, culture, and fashion, a cauldron of the intellectual avant-garde. But it is also a city of well-tended gardens, of cafés highly suited to people-watching, a feast of grand architectural splendors and small delights around every corner. And speaking of feasts, the food's not bad, either!

Paris is best seen on foot, walking up and down narrow passages and wide boulevards. With map in hand, it's hard to get lost. But what a treat it is to meander through the streets, taking in unexpected pleasures at nearly every step.

We encourage you to do just that: wander the streets as you visit the sites in this guidebook. There are so many extraordinary places in Paris that we've kept to our favorites, those exemplifying Paris as a center of style and re-invention, both historically and today. By exploring the city you'll discover what you love most.

Paris is divided into numbered sectors called "*arrondissements*," postal codes by which Parisians identify locations. However, we've arranged this guidebook by clusters of neighborhoods, or quarters. (You will find that we have included the *arrondissements* within the specific addresses of sites.) The first seven chapters cover such clusters in central Paris, each with its own map. The eighth chapter highlights places on the city's outskirts, and the ninth chapter includes short excursions to spots near Paris. We've also included an overview map of the entire city inside the front cover and a public transportation map in the back.

Once you've explored Paris and been enchanted by its beauty and spirit, you can quote Humphrey Bogart when, in the movie *Casablanca*, he tells Ingrid Bergman, "We'll always have Paris."

GREAT VIEWS

For the best—and it's free!—sightseeing tour, walk along the Seine River. The views are spectacular. Be sure to look down at the walkways bordering the water: you'll see lovers kissing beneath the trees, students poring over books, fishermen patiently holding a line in the water, and the occasional beret-topped *grand-père* calmly feeding the pigeons.

You'll find other great views from atop the Eiffel Tower, the steps and terraces of Sacré-Coeur, the Georges restaurant on the roof of Beaubourg (Centre Georges Pompidou), the roof of the Institute of the Arab World, and, following in the footsteps of Quasimodo, the North Tower of Notre Dame.

For a river view, ride a tourist boat *(bateau-mouche)* along the Seine. **Bateaux-Mouches** depart from the Alma Bridge *(T. 01-42.25.96.10, www.bateaux-mouches.fr).* **Bateaux Parisiens** depart from Port de la Bourdonnais, near the Eiffel Tower *(T. 01-46.99.43.13, www.bateaux parisiens.com).* **Vedettes du Pont-Neuf** *(Square du Vert Galant, Paris 1st, T. 01-46.33.98.38, www.vedettes dupontneuf.com)* are open boats. Or catch the **Batobus** *(T. 08-25.05.01.01, www.batobus.com)*, public transportation on the river, at any of its eight stops between the Eiffel Tower and the Jardin des Plantes.

HOW TO USE THIS GUIDE

We have included a map for each neighborhood with color-coded numbers corresponding to the places mentioned in the text. **Red** symbols indicate **Places to See** (landmarks and arts & entertainment). **Blue** symbols indicate **Places to Eat & Drink** (restaurants, cafés, bars, and nightlife). **Orange** symbols indicate **Where to Shop**. **Green** symbols indicate **Where to Stay**. Some restaurants are closed in August, so check before going.

Here are our keys for restaurant and hotel costs:

Restaurants

Cost of an appetizer and main course without drinks

(€)	Up to 25€
(€€)	25€-50€
(€€€)	50€-75€
(€€€€)	75€ and up

Hotels

Cost per night

(€)	Up to 150€
(€€)	150€-250€
(€€€)	250€-400€
(€€€€)	400€ and up

Abbreviations

M métro (subway) station

ALL ABOUT MONEY

Money changing

The currency in France is Euros (€). ATMs abound and most places take credit cards. Visa is commonly called "Carte Bleue" and MasterCard is often referred to as "Eurocard." Exchange rates for cash or travelers' checks are best in banks, but some offer the service for their clients only. Avoid changing money in airports, train stations, hotels, restaurants, and shops. You can try these places:

AMERICAN EXPRESS: 11 rue Scribe, 9th *(M: Opéra, exit rue Scribe, T. 01-47.77.79.50)*

CITIBANK: 125 avénue Champs-Elysées, 8th *(M: Charles-de-Gaulle-Etoile, T. 01-53.23.33.60)*

COMPTOIR DE CHANGE OPÉRA: 9 rue Scribe, 9th *(M: Opéra, T. 01-47.42.20.96)*

MULTICHANGE: 7 rue de Castiglione, 1st (and other locations) *(M: Tuileries, T. 01-40.15.61.16, www.multi-change.com)*

Tipping

A 15% service charge is added to all hotel and restaurant bills in France. But sometimes an additional tip is appropriate. A few extra Euro-cents in a bar or café is fine; up to 10% in a restaurant if the waiter was particularly good. In hotels, tip 1€/bag for bellboys, 1€ for room service, 1€/day for housekeeping. For taxi drivers, tip 10%–15% on meter fares. In hair salons, give 10%–15% for any service.

Got cents?

Decimal points and commas are reversed from the U.S. system. So Euros are separated from Euro-cents *(centimes)* by a comma, and hundreds are separated from thousands by a period. On price tags, a € sign often replaces the decimal point (8,50€ = 8€50).

PUBLIC TRANSPORTATION

Getting to and from the Airport

Paris's two major airports are Roissy/Charles de Gaulle (CDG) and Orly. Flights from the U.S. generally go to CDG. Free shuttle buses marked "ADP" (Aéroports de Paris) connect the terminals and go to the Roissy RER (regional rapid-transit train/subway) station. The airport RER costs about 9€ one way.

Taxis into town cost about 65€ during off-hours, more at peak hours. Car and van services require reservations (16€–20€ per person). Aéroport Limousine Service *(T. 01-40.71.84.62)* is a fixed-fare car service. Airport

Connection *(T. 01-44.18.36.02)* is a door-to-door minibus service. Airport Shuttle is another van service *(toll-free: 0-800-699-699)*.

Non-reservation buses include the Air France Bus, about 12€ *(T. 01-41.56.89.00, recording in French and English)*, and RoissyBus, the RATP city bus, about 9€ *(T. 01-48.04.18.24)*.

More information on getting into the city is available at:
www.parisnet.net/info_airplane.html
www.parisnet.net/parishuttle.html
www.paris.org/Accueil/Airport
www.worldairportguide.co.uk/airports/cdg/cdg.asp
www.paris-cdg.com

Métro, RER, SNCF, and Travel Passes

"Le Métro" is the subway. Individual métro/bus tickets cost 1€40, and a book of 10 tickets *(carnet)* costs 10€70. Visitors' passes are also sold at métro stations and online. Métro lines are identified by different numbers and colors. There is a fold-out Paris métro map in the back of this book. The métro runs daily from 5:30 AM to 12:40 AM.

The **RER** is a system of commuter trains that transports people from the outskirts of Paris into the central city. Many of the stations overlap with the métro stations and can be used interchangeably (tickets and passes are valid for both within the city). There are five different lines (A, B, C, D, and E), each with a different color. These are indicated on the map in the back of the book with slightly thicker lines than the métro lines. In some cases, it might be quicker to use an RER train to get from one destination to another because there will be fewer stops in between, than on the métro train. The RER trains run daily from 5:30 AM to 1:00 AM.

There are five **SNCF** *(reservations and information: 08-92.35.35.35, open daily 7 AM to 10 PM, www.sncf.com)* rail train stations that travel much further out of the city. These can be used for long-distance destinations and excursions. The station names appear in boldface type in the map at the back of the book, and the lines are a light gray color. You would use these for destinations featured in Chapter 9.

Paris Visite is a pass for 1, 2, 3, or 5 consecutive days of unlimited travel on the métro or buses *(www.paris visite.com/en/index.php)*. Some passes are for Paris only; others include outskirts.

PHONE NUMBER, S'IL VOUS PLAÎT?

When calling Paris direct from the U.S., dial 011-33 then drop the initial 0 in the number. When dialing within France or within Paris, dial the number as it appears (with the initial 0).

SHOPPING

Opening hours: We have included specific store hours wherever possible in this guide. As a general rule, Paris shops are usually open Monday through Saturday from 10AM to 7PM. But there are exceptions. Some shops are open on Sundays. Markets and neighborhood stores may be closed on Mondays. Boutiques often close for lunch, and small shops close for vacation, usually in August.

Sales: By law, sales *(soldes)* are held twice a year in France, in January and July. In Paris they last a month. At other times of year, good deals are marked in stores as *"promotions."*

Tax refunds: If you spend a minimum of 175€ in one store, you can get a tax refund *(détaxe)*. You must show your passport and fill out a form in the store. On leaving at the airport, go to the *"bureau de détaxe"* to get your forms stamped. Do this before going through passport control or baggage check-in: you may have to show your purchases. Back home, return the pink copy in the envelope provided; keep the other for your records. If traveling to other EU countries, get your forms stamped in the airport customs office of the last EU country you leave. It takes about three months to get the refund.

Duty-free shops: Best at airports. The duty-free shops around Opéra and Palais Royal aren't much of a deal.

Chain and discount stores: Fnac is a chain store great for books, CDs, and electronics. Paris's main discount chain stores are Prisunic and Monoprix.

SAY IT IN FRENCH

Although it's best to carry a phrase book, here are a few basic words and phrases to get you started.

Bonjour *(bohn-zhOOR)* Hello; good morning/day
Bon soir *(bohn sWAH)* Good evening
Au revoir *(or-vwAR)* Good-bye
S'il vous plaît *(sill voo plEH)* Please
Je voudrais… *(zhuh voo-DRAY)* I would like …
Merci *(mare-sEE)* Thank you
Oui *(wEE)* Yes
Non *(nOH)* No
Où est… *(oo ay…)* Where is …
le métro *(luh meh-tRO)* subway
un carnet *(un car-nAY)* packet of 10 subway tickets
un billet *(un bee-yAY)* ticket
la rue *(lah rOO)* street
l'hôtel *(low-tEL)* hotel; house/mansion
le magasin *(magazEHN)* store
le grand magasin *(gran magazEHN)* department store
le restaurant *(restorON)* restaurant
Parlez-vous anglais? *(par-lay voo ohng-LAY)*
   Do you speak English?
Où sont les toilettes? *(oo sohn les twalET?)*
   Where is the bathroom?
Ça coûte combien? *(Sah koot kombee-EN?)*
   How much does that cost?
Madame *(mah-dAHM)* Ma'am; Mrs.
Mademoiselle *(mahd-mwa-zEL)* Miss
Monsieur *(muss-YUH)* Sir; Mr.

ETIQUETTE TIP

Whether it's "Bonjour," "Au revoir," "Merci," or "S'il vous plaît," it's rude to address someone without saying "Madame" or "Monsieur" after the address. On entering a shop, always first say, "Bonjour, Madame/Monsieur." If you enter a store with a man and a woman clerk, greet both with, "Bonjour, Madame, Monsieur." Even the surliest Parisian waiter will say hello! Just don't call him "garçon"—it means both "waiter" and "boy" and is considered rude. Better to say, "S'il vous plaît, Monsieur."

BOOKING TICKETS

You can buy theatre and concert tickets at any **Fnac** *(one branch is at 74 ave. des Champs-Elysées, 8th, M: George V, T. 01-53.53.64.64, wwwfnac.com; hours: M–Sa 10AM–12AM, Su 12PM–12AM)* or **Virgin Megastore** *(52–60 ave. des Champs-Elysées, 8th, M: Franklin D. Roosevelt, T. 01-49.53.50.00; hours: M–Sa 10AM–12AM, Su 12PM–12AM)*, and also at **Carrousel du Louvre** *(99 rue de Rivoli, M: Concorde, T. 01-44.50-03-10; hours: M–Su 9AM–10PM)*. Same-day, half-price tickets (commercial fare) sell at **Kiosque de la Madeleine** *(15 pl. de la Madeleine, 8th, M: Madeleine or Concorde; hours: Tu–Sa 12:30PM–7:45PM, Sun 12:30PM–3:45PM)*. Most theatres are closed on Mondays. Magazines with listings for arts and entertainment are available at newsstands—in French, every Wednesday; *Pariscope*; *L'Officiel des Spectacles*; and *Zurban*; in English: *Paris Free Voice* and *The City* (quarterly).

Paris Museum is a pass for 1, 3, or 5 consecutive days of unlimited visits to museums (permanent collections) and monuments. Kids under 18 enter most museums free; those 18 to 25 years old at reduced rates. See the following Web sites for more information:
www.museums-of-paris.com/museum-pass.php
www.conciergerie.com
www.discoverfrance.net

SEASONAL EVENTS

Winter-Spring:

Salon des Grands Vins, early Feb., wine tastings & workshops *(Carrousel du Louvre, 99 rue de Rivoli, 1st, M: Palais Royal, www.salondesgrandsvins.com)*

Printemps des Poètes, Mar., national poetry festival *(various venues, www.printempsdespoetes.com)*

Paris Film Festival, April *(various venues, T. 01-45.72. 96.40, www.festivaldufilmdeparis.com)*

Summer:

French Tennis Open, May-June *(Stade Roland Garros, 2 ave. Gordon-Bennett, 16th, M: Porte d'Auteuil, T. 01-47.43.48.00, www.frenchopen.org)*

Quinzaine des Réalisateurs, May-June, films from the Cannes Festival *(Forum des Images, Porte St-Eustache, Forum des Halles, 1st, M: Les Halles, T. 01-44.76.62.00, www.forumdesimages.net)*

Paris Jazz Festival, June-July *(Parc Floral de Paris, Bois de Vincennes, 12th, M: Château de Vincennes, T. 08-20. 00.75.75, www.parcfloraldeparis.com)*

Gay Pride March, last Sat. in June *(Centre Gai et Lesbien, 11th, T. 01-43.57.21.47, www.fiertes-lgbt.org)*

Bastille Day, July 14, celebration of French Revolution, dancing at pl. de la Bastille on eve, parade in morning, fireworks at Champ de Mars at night

Paris-Plage, mid-July to mid-Aug., sandy beach along the Seine *(T. 08-20.00.75.75, www.paris.fr)*

Tour de France, July, ends at Champs-Elysées *(T. 01-41. 33.15.00, www.letour.fr)*

Autumn:

Villette Jazz Festival, early Sept. *(Parc de la Villette, 211 ave. Jean-Jaurès, 19th, M: Porte de Pantin, T. 01-40.03. 75.75, www.villette.com)*

Nuit Blanche ("All-Nighter"), early Oct., galleries, museums, bars, clubs open all night *(T. 08-20.00.75.75, www.paris.fr)*

FIAC, end Oct., international art fair *(Paris-Expo, Porte de Versailles, 15th, M: Porte de Versailles, T. 01-41.90. 47.80, www.fiac-online.com)*

Fête du Beaujolais Nouveau, 3rd Thurs. in Nov., new vintage, wine tastings throughout the city

Africolor, mid-Dec., African music festival *(various venues in St-Denis, M: Basilique de St-Denis, T. 01-47.97. 69.99, www.africolor.com)*

PARIS'S TOP PICKS

Paris offers an abundance of one-of-a-kind attractions for visitors. Here are 11 of the top picks not to be missed!

- ★ **Eiffel Tower** *(see page 24)*
- ★ **Arc de Triomphe** *(see page 32)*
- ★ **Place de la Concorde** *(see page 33)*
- ★ **Opéra Garnier** *(see page 44)*
- ★ **Louvre Museum** *(see page 50)*
- ★ **Centre Georges Pompidou** *(see page 77)*
- ★ **Sainte-Chapelle** *(see page 125)*
- ★ **Notre-Dame** *(see page 126)*
- ★ **Jardin de Luxembourg** *(see page 139)*
- ★ **Musée d'Orsay** *(see page 152)*
- ★ **Sacré-Coeur** *(see page 170)*

chapter 1

INVALIDES

CHAILLOT

CHAMPS-ELYSÉES

INVALIDES
CHAILLOT
CHAMPS-ELYSÉES

Places to See:

1. Pont Alexandre III
2. Hôtel des Invalides
3. Assemblée Nationale
4. Hôtel Matignon
5. EIFFEL TOWER ★
6. Rodin Museum
7. Sewers
8. La Pagode
20. Palais de Chaillot
21. Trocadéro Gardens
22. Musée du Vin
23. Musée Guimet
24. Palais de Tokyo
25. Palais Galliéra Fashion Museum
26. Maison de Radio-France
35. ARC DE TRIOMPHE ★
36. Grand Palais
37. Petit Palais
38. Elysée Palace
39. PLACE DE LA CONCORDE ★
40. Atelier Renault
41. Théâtre des Champs-Elysées
42. L'Atelier des Chefs
43. Musée Jacquemart-André

Places to Eat & Drink:

9. Aux Ducs de Bourgogne
10. Bistrot le P'tit Troquet
11. Jules Verne
12. Café Constant
13. Les Fables de la Fontaine
14. Le Violon d'Ingres
27. L'Astrance
28. La Table de Joël Robuchon
29. Cristal Room
30. Tokyo Eat
44. Boutiques Vignon
45. Atelier Renault Café/Bar
46. Pierre Gagnaire
47. Restaurant Guy Savoy
48. Monte Carlo Restaurant Buffet
49. BE Boulangépicier
50. L'Écluse François-1er
51. Nirvana

Where to Shop:

15. Loulou de la Falaise
16. Maison Poujauran
31. Avenue Victor Hugo
53. Inès de la Fressange
54. D. Porthault
55. Fouquet

★ Top Picks

If you are lucky enough to have lived in Paris as a young man, then wherever you go for the rest of your life, it stays with you, for Paris is a moveable feast.

—*Ernest Hemingway*

INVALIDES

8 **13** *to Invalides;* **12** *to Assemblée Nationale;*
13 *to Varenne;* **8** *to École Militaire;*
6 *to Bir Hakeim (Tour Eiffel)*

• SNAPSHOT •

Over its colorful history, Invalides has been refuge to
torn and tattered soldiers, a tool of rebellious crowds,
and home to Napoleon's tomb. From monuments to
government buildings to 18th-century aristocratic town
houses, the Invalides area exudes *hauteur* and beauty on
a grand scale. It is the Left (southern) Bank's equivalent
of Right (northern) Bank grandeur. It's home to the
renowned Eiffel Tower, the magnificent Rodin
Museum, and other "not-to-be-missed" sites.

PLACES TO SEE
Landmarks:

The Art Nouveau lamps of the ornate, exuberant **Pont
Alexandre III (1)** *(off of ave. du Maréchal-Gallieni, 8th)*
create an elegant curve bridging the Seine River. The
gilded statuary—cherubs, nymphs, and winged horses
—of this flamboyant bridge leads directly to the **Hôtel
des Invalides (2)** *(Esplanade des Invalides,
7th, 01-44.42.37.72, www.invalides.org;
hours: Oct–Mar 10AM–5PM; Apr–Sept
10AM–6PM; closed 1st M of month, Jan 1,
May 1, Nov 1, Dec 25)* on the Left Bank.
Commissioned by Louis XIV as a hospi-

tal for French soldiers, Invalides now houses several military museums, notably the **Musée de l'Armée** and **Napoleon's Tomb** (under the gilded baroque dome). East of Invalides, along the Seine, is the **Assemblée Nationale (3)**, or Palais Bourbon *(33 quai d'Orsay, 7th, 01-40.63.00.00, www.assemblee-nat.fr)*, the lower body of the French parliament. The Prime Minister resides at the **Hôtel Matignon (4)** *(57 rue de Varenne, 7th, closed to public)*.

On the other (west) side of Invalides is the **École Militaire** with its vast training ground, the **Champ de Mars** (great for jogging). At the far end of this park, bordering the Seine, is Paris's most renowned sight, the cast-iron

★**EIFFEL TOWER (5)** *(Champ de Mars, 7th, 01-44.11.23.23, www.tour-eiffel.fr; hours: Jan–June 12, Sept–Dec 9:30AM–11PM; June 13–Aug 9AM–12AM)*. Built for the 1889 World's Fair and the centennial of the French Revolution, the *Tour Eiffel* was condemned in its time as an eyesore, called both a "belfry skeleton" and a "truly

tragic street lamp." Guy de Maupassant said it was a "high and skinny pyramid of iron ladders … which just peters out into a ridiculous thin shape like a factory chimney." Some claimed they lunched there to avoid looking at it. Still, two million people visited the tower in 1889; less than a century later, it had become perhaps the most beloved symbol of Paris. Observation platforms at all three levels provide spectacular views, next to souvenir shops, cafés, and exhibitions. The stunning night view of Paris from the Eiffel Tower may leave you breathless; and for ten minutes every hour a dazzling 20,000-bulb light show makes the ironwork seem magical.

Arts & Entertainment:

The **Rodin Museum (6)** *(77 rue de Varenne, 7th, 01-44. 18.61.10, www.musee-rodin.fr; hours: Apr–Sept 9:30AM– 5:45PM; Oct–Mar 9:30AM–4:45PM, closed M)* is one of the best in Paris, with Auguste Rodin's great sculptures on display both inside and in the garden outside. Don't miss *The Kiss*, *The Thinker*, *Balzac*, *The Gates of Hell*, and *The Burghers of Calais*. For a unique underground museum, pop into the **Sewers (7)** *(Égouts de Paris, opposite 93 quai d'Orsay, off the Alma Bridge, 7th, 01-53. 68.27.81; hours: winter Sa–W 11AM–4PM; summer Sa–W 11AM–5PM)*. If you're in the mood for a non-mainstream film, **La Pagode (8)** *(57 bis, rue de Babylone, 7th, 08-92.89.28.92)* shows international independent films.

PLACES TO EAT & DRINK

Lunch at the cozy *crêperie* **Aux Ducs de Bourgogne (9)** *(€)* *(30 rue de Bourgogne, 7th, 01-45.51.32.48, lunch only)* or order take-outs. The intimate **Bistrot le P'tit Troquet (10)** *(€€)* *(28 rue de l'Exposition, 7th, 01-47.05.80.39; call for hours)* serves traditional French food. The food and the views at **Jules Verne**

(11) *(€€€€)* *(Eiffel Tower, Level 2, 7th, 01-45.55.61.44; hours: 12:15PM–1:45PM, 7:15PM–9:45PM, book ahead)* are fabulous, but the less expensive **Eiffel Tower (5)** cafés have the same vista. Chef Christian Constant boasts three restaurants in the area: **Café Constant (12)** *(€€)* *(139 rue St-Dominique, 7th, 01-47.53.73.34, www.leviolondingres.com; hours: 8:30AM breakfast, 12PM–2:30PM, 7PM–10:30PM, drinks all day)*, **Les Fables de la Fontaine (13)** *(€€)* *(131 rue St-Dominique, 7th, 01-44.18.37.55, www.leviolon dingres.com; hours: 12PM–2:30PM, 7:15PM–11PM)* for seafood, and the exquisite **Le Violon d'Ingres (14)** *(€€)* *(135 rue St-Dominique, 7th, 01-45.55.15.05, www.levi olondingres.com; hours: Tu–Sa 12PM–2:30PM, 7PM–10:30PM)*.

WHERE TO SHOP

The boutique of designer **Loulou de la Falaise (15)** *(7 rue de Bourgogne, 7th, 01-45.51.42.22, www.loulou-de-la-falaise.com)* is awash in vibrantly colored, imaginative clothes and accessories. At **Maison Poujauran (16)** *(18-20 rue Jean-Nicot, 7th, 01-47.05.80.88)*, a tiny old-fashioned *boulangerie*, you'll find wonderful *baguettes* and biscuits *(sablés)*; it's the official bread supplier to the Elysée Palace, the presidential residence—credentials well-earned. **Jeanne et Jéremy (70)** *(Village Suisse, 78 ave. de Suffren, 15th, www.jeannejeremy.com; hours: Th–Sa 11AM–7PM, Su 2PM–7PM)* is a teddy bear heaven; these not-so-stuffy creatures are designed by artists.

WHERE TO STAY

Practical, minimalist rooms make **Grand Hôtel Lévêque (17)** (€) *(29 rue Cler, 7th, 01-47.05.49.15, www.hotel-lev eque.com)* a low-budget favorite. For elegance and luxury in the diplomatic neighborhood around parliament, **Bourgogne & Montana (18)** (€€-€€€) *(3 rue de Bourgogne, 7th, 01-45.51.20.22, toll-free from US 800-44-UTELL, www.bourgogne-montana.com)* exudes tradition for a classy clientele. Quiet and hospitable, **Hôtel de Londres Eiffel (19)** (€€) *(1 rue Augereau, 7th, 01-45.51.63.02, www.londres-eiffel.com)* is tastefully outfitted.

CHAILLOT

6 **9** to Trocadéro; **9** to Iéna or Alma-Marceau;
2 to Victor Hugo; **1** **2** **6** to Ch. de Gaulle-Étoile

• SNAPSHOT •

"Opulent" and "staid" best describe the exclusive Chaillot quarter. The village of Chaillot was annexed into Paris and underwent surgery during the modernizations of Baron Haussmann, under Napoleon III, to become a neighborhood of grandeur for the *haute bourgeoisie*. It is arguably one of the best places in Paris to catch phenomenal views of the city and its treasures.

PLACES TO SEE
Landmarks:

Facing the Eiffel Tower, across the Seine past the Iéna Bridge, is the monumental **Palais de Chaillot (20)** *(17 pl. du Trocadéro, 16th)*. Its two curved Neoclassical wings,

harsh and cumbersome, provide great photo ops from the central terrace: a magnificent view of the river and the Eiffel Tower. The **Trocadéro Gardens (21)** *(16th)* sweep down from the terrace, around a long, central pool of fountains bordered by statues.

Arts & Entertainment:

The **Palais de Chaillot (20)** *(see also "Places to See")* houses several museums: for architecture, the **Cité de l'Architecture et du Patrimoine** *(01-*

44.05.39.10, www.citechaillot.fr; hours: M, W, F–Su 11AM–7PM, Th 11AM–9PM); for anthropology and archaeology, the **Musée de l'Homme** (01-44.05.72.72, www.mnhn.fr; hours: M, W–F 10AM–5PM, Sa–Su 10AM–6PM); and for French mar-

itime history, the **Musée de la Marine** (01-53.65.69.69, www.musee-marine.fr; hours: W–M 10AM–6PM). For the history of winemaking (and tastings), visit the **Musée du Vin (22)** (rue des Eaux, 16th, 01-45.25.63.26, www.museeduvinparis.com; hours: Tu–Su 10AM–6PM). The **Théâtre National de Chaillot** (01-53.65.31.00) in the **Palais de Chaillot (20)** (see also page 28) stages classics and some musicals. Nearby is the **Musée Guimet (23)** (6 pl. d'Iéna, 16th, 01-56.52.53.00, www.museeguimet.fr; hours: W–M 10AM–6PM), one of the world's major muse-ums of Asian art. The Neoclassical **Palais de Tokyo (24)** (13 ave. du Président-Wilson, 16th, 01-47.23.38.86, www.palaisdetokyo.com; hours: Tu–Su 12PM–12AM) is notable for its stunningly redesigned interior. It houses the **Museum of Modern Art** in the east wing and the **Site de Création Contemporaine** in the west wing. Versatile, dynamic, and imaginative, the space morphs for each exhibit's needs. The café terrace affords a great view of the Seine. Paris fashion shows are by invitation only, but the **Palais Galliéra Fashion Museum (25)** (Musée de la Mode et du Costume, Palais Galliéra, 10 ave. Pierre 1er de Serbie, 16th, 01-56.52.86.20; hours: W–M 10AM–6PM) holds two or three French fashion exhibits per year. Free concerts at **Maison de Radio-France (26)**

(116 ave. du Président-Kennedy, 16th, 01-53.92.01.23, www.radiofrance.fr; call for concert times) feature classical music and well-known popular musicians.

PLACES TO EAT & DRINK
Where to Eat:

Celebrity chef Pascal Barbot's culinary creations at **L'Astrance (27)** (€€€) *(4 rue Beethoven, 16th, 01-40.50.84.40; hours: Tu–F 12:30PM–1:30PM, 8:30PM–11:45PM, Sa 8:30PM–11:45PM)* are superb; it's tiny, so book months in advance. Equally *magnifique* is **La Table de Joël Robuchon (28)** (€€€) *(16 ave. Bugeaud, 16th, 01-56.28.16.16, www.joel-robuchon.com; hours: 12PM–2:30PM, 7PM–11PM).* For a trip into surreal fantasy, the Philippe Starck–designed **Cristal Room (29)** (€€€€) *(11 pl. des Étas-Unis, 16th, 01-40.22.11.10, www.baccarat.fr; hours: M–Sa 12PM–2PM, 7:30PM– 10PM, reserve 1 month ahead; M–F 8:30AM–10AM, Sa 10AM, tea Sa 3PM–5PM)* is very hot. The décor reflects the eccentricity of the mansion's former owner, Marie-Laure de Noailles, friend of Cocteau, Dalí, Man Ray, and Buñuel. Or opt for a sandwich at one of the many elegant cafés on the Place du Trocadéro. The postmodern **Tokyo Eat (30)** (€€) *(Palais de Tokyo, 13 ave. du Président-Wilson, 16th, 01-47.20.00.29; hours: Tu–Su 12PM–1AM),* the restaurant at the **Palais de Tokyo (24)** *(see also page 29)*, is as much an artistic and aesthetically pleasing experience as it is a culinary one.

Bars & Nightlife:

This staid neighborhood isn't known for nightlife. But there's a cultural night scene at the **Palais de Tokyo (24)** *(see also page 29)*, whose fabulous exhibits of international art are open until midnight.

WHERE TO SHOP

A host of fashion designers display their work in boutiques along Avenue Victor Hugo (31), among them **Apostrophe** *(No. 5)*. The style strength of this particular avenue can best be described in two words: conservative and classic.

WHERE TO STAY

This area is not very exciting for tourists; it is well suited for business travelers. For casual French chic, **Au Palais de Chaillot Hôtel (32)** (€) *(35 ave. Raymond Poincaré, 16th, 01-53.70.09.09, www.chaillotel.com)* offers bang for the buck. The rooms at **Hôtel du Rond-Point de Longchamp (33)** (€€€) *(86 rue de Longchamp, at pl. de Mexico, 16th, 01-45.05.13.63, www.rd-pt-longchamp.fr)* vary in décor from Louis XIV to efficiently modern.

CHAMPS-ELYSÉES

(1) (2) (6) *to Ch. de Gaulle-Étoile;*
(1) *to George V or FDR;* (9) *to Alma Marceau;*
(1) (13) *to Champs-Élysées-Clemenceau;*
(1) (8) (12) *to Concorde*

• SNAPSHOT •

The Champs-Elysées district and the Place Charles-de-Gaulle (or Place de l'Étoile) epitomize the spirit of the *grands boulevards*. Twelve wide avenues radiate from the rotary of l'Étoile ("star"), cutting a grandiose swath through majestic *fin-de-siècle* residences. Despite the infiltration of commercialism on Champs-Elysées Avenue, the quarter is among the city's most aristocratic—and among the most popular for tourists who wish to take in perhaps the most famous avenue of the city. But the area is not just a tourist spot—it hosts numerous events and spectacular displays of national pride on days such as Bastille Day and New Year's Eve.

PLACES TO SEE
Landmarks:

In the center of Étoile, an island in a sea of moving vehicles, towers the **★ARC DE TRIOMPHE (35)** *(pl. Charles-de-Gaulle/Étoile, 8th, 01-55.37.73.77).* Commissioned by Napoleon, the enormous, 164-foot-tall structure was to be a triumphal gateway for the emperor's returning armies. Instead, in 1840, four years after the building's completion, Napoleon's ashes passed beneath the arch on the way to his tomb in Les Invalides. Victorious French soldiers finally marched through the arch at the end of WWI. Beneath it lies the Tomb of the Unknown Soldier. Once the focus of fashionable society, the **Avenue des Champs-Elysées** has lost much of its aristocratic cachet but remains Paris's most famous street. The **Grand Palais (36)** *(Porte A, ave. Général-Eisenhower, 8th, 01-44.13.17.30; hours: W 10AM–10PM, Th–M 10AM–8PM)*, an imposing exhibition hall with a magnificent glass-roofed central atrium, mixes classical stonework with Art Nouveau ironwork, topped with galloping bronze horses. Architecturally similar, the **Petit Palais (37)** *(ave. Winston Churchill, 8th, 01-44.51.19.31; hours: Tu–Su 10AM–6PM)* exhibits the city's collection of French and Renaissance art. Its dome mirrors the Invalides cupola directly across the river. North of the Champs-Elysées, the beautiful **Elysée Palace (38)** *(55 rue du Faubourg-St-Honoré, 8th, closed to the public)*, with its English gardens, is the official residence of the president of the Republic. At the eastern end of the Champs-Elysées, the

TOP PICK!

★PLACE DE LA CONCORDE (39) *(8th)*, with its beautiful fountains, was built in 1750 with a grand statue of Louis XV in the center. During the French Revolution, the statue was dismantled and a guillotine set up in its place: Louis XVI, Marie-Antoinette, Robespierre, Danton, along with more than 1,000 others, all lost their heads here. Concorde, Paris's largest square, is a focal point for surrounding major landmarks: the **Arc de Triomphe (35)** (west) *(see also page 32)*, the **Madeleine church** (north), the **National Assembly** (south), and the **Tuileries Gardens** and **Louvre** (east). At the center of the square is a wonderful gift from Egypt— a 75-foot-tall **obelisk**, covered in hieroglyphics, from the temple of Luxor.

Arts & Entertainment:

Besides the museums mentioned earlier, it's fun to visit the **Atelier Renault (40)** *(53 ave. des Champs-Elysées, 8th, 01-49.53.70.70, www.atelier-renault.com; hours: Su–Th 10:30AM–12:30AM, F–Sa 10:30AM–2:30AM)*, where cars aren't only on the showroom floor, they're on the walls, too. The top classical music and opera concert venue is the **Théâtre des Champs-Elysées (41)** *(15 ave. Montaigne, 8th, 01-49.52.50.50, www.theatrechampselysees.fr; call for show times)*. Or take a cooking class at **L'Atelier des Chefs (42)** *(10 rue de Penthièvre, 8th, 01-53.30.05.82, www.latelierdeschefs. com; call for course times)* in a glass-roofed loft. **Musée Jacquemart-André (43)** *(158 bd. Haussmann, 8th, 01-45.62.11.59, www.musee-jacquemart-andre. com; hours: 10AM–6PM)*, once the home of banker

Édouard André and portraitist Nélie Jacquemart, is an extravagant jewel containing an extraordinary collection of paintings, tapestries, and furniture.

PLACES TO EAT & DRINK
Where to Eat:

Find gourmet take-out at **Boutiques Vignon (44)** (€) *(14 rue Marbeuf, 8th, 01-47.20.24.26; call for hours).*

Drugstore Publicis (59) (€€) *(133 ave. des Champs-Elysées, 8th, 01-47.20.39.25; hours: M–F 8AM–2AM, Sa–Su 10AM–2AM),* good for a quick bite, is a stylish general store with restaurants and a pharmacy. The **Atelier Renault Café/Bar (45)** (€–€€) *(53 ave. des Champs-Elysées, 8th, 01-49.53.70.70, www. atelier-renault.com; hours: Su–Th 10:30AM–12:30AM, F–Sa 10:30AM–2:30AM) (see also page 34)* is a perfect people-watching place. An avant-garde, extravagant food experience for gourmets, **Pierre Gagnaire (46)** (€€€) *(Hôtel Balzac, 6 rue Balzac, 8th, 01-58.36.12.50, www.pierre-gagnaire.com; hours: M–Tu, Th–F 12PM–1:30PM, 7:30PM–10PM, W 7:30PM–10PM, Su 7:30PM–10PM, closed first 2 wks Aug)* dazzles as it delights. **Restaurant Guy Savoy (47)** (€€€€) *(18 rue Troyon, 17th, 01-43.80.40.61, www.guysavoy.com; hours: Tu–F 12PM–2PM, 7PM–10:30PM, Sa 7PM–10:30PM)* combines country inn hospitality with sensuous gastronomy. The cafeteria-style self-service at **Monte Carlo Restaurant Buffet (48)** (€) *(9 ave. de Wagram, 17th, 01-43.80.02.20/21; call for hours)* is a great bargain for the area. It has many dishes to choose from and even comes with wine. Celebrity chef Alain Ducasse does gourmet sandwiches in his deli/bread shop **BE Boulangépicier (49) (€)** *(73 bd. de Courcelles, 17th, 01-46.22.20.20, www.boulangepicier.com; hours: M–Sa 7AM–8PM).*

Bars & Nightlife:

With a wide selection of wines to sample, along with seasonal French dishes, **L'Écluse François-1er (50)** *(64 rue François 1er, 8th, 01-47.20.77.09, www.lecluse baravin.com; call for hours)* is a trendy wine bar. There's a line to get into the hip club **Nirvana (51)** *(3 ave. Matignon, 8th, 01-53.89.18.91; hours: open to 5AM)*, but it's friendly, and the dance floor rocks (the restaurant is expensive).

WHERE TO SHOP

In and around the triangle of **avenues George V, Champs-Elysées**, and **Montaigne** is an embarrassment of riches, overflowing with designer fashion houses. You'll find women's wear at Inès de la Fressange (53) *(31 ave. Franklin D. Roosevelt, 8th, 01-56.88.34.00)* (she's the official face of France, traditionally called "Marianne"), and French linens at D. Porthault (54) *(18 ave. Montaigne, 8th, 01-47.20.75.25)*. For specialty foodstuffs, Fouquet (55) *(22 rue François 1er, 8th, 01-47.23.30.36, www.fouquet.fr)* is a dream.

Men's shirts and neckties are the focus at Alain Figaret (57) *(14 bis rue Marbeuf, 8th, 01-47.23.35.49 www.alain-figaret.com)*; hats fill Motsch et Fils (58) *(42 ave. George V, 8th, 01-47.23.79.22)*. There's everything from toys to books to shampoo at Drugstore Publicis (59) *(133 ave. des Champs-Elysées, 8th, 0147.20.39.25; hours: 8AM–2AM)*. The chain store Monoprix (60) *(Branch at 52 ave. des Champs-Elysées, 8th, 01-53.77.65.65; hours: M–Sa 9AM–12AM)* has a variety of good inexpensive items. Next door the Virgin Megastore (61) *(52-60 ave. des Champs-Elysées, 8th, 01-40. 74. 06.48; hours: M–Sa 10AM–12AM, Su 12PM–12AM)* sells CDs, books, and electronics.

Expensive art and antiques galleries line **Avenue Matignon**, as well as a stamp and postcard collectors' market. Artcurial

(62) (*7 rond-point des Champs-Elysées, 8th, 01-42 .99.16.20, www.artcurial.com; hours: M–Sa 10:30AM– 7PM*) boasts one of the largest collections of art books in Paris. The **rue du Faubourg St-Honoré** (and its continuation rue St-Honoré) is Paris's most famous street for shopping. *Prêt-à-porter* designer shops abound along with places such as the

Anne Sémonin (63) (*Hôtel Le Bristol, 108 rue du Faubourg St-Honoré, 8th, 01-42.66.24.22, www.anne semonin.com*) day spa and **Anna Lowe (65)** (*104 rue du Faubourg St-Honoré, 8th, 01-42.66.11.32, www. annalowe.com*), which offers savings of about 40% on off-the-runway women's designer clothes. Down the street, legendary **Roger Vivier (64)** (*29 rue du Faubourg-St-Honoré, 8th, 01-53.43.00.85, www.roger vivier.com*) shoes are like foot sculpture from the inventor of stiletto heels.

WHERE TO STAY

Luxurious **Hôtel Plaza Athénée (67)** (€€€€) (*25 ave. Montaigne, 8th, 01-53.67.66.65, www.plaza-athenee-paris.com*) is a legend, drawing fashionistas, honeymooners, and aristocracy alike. The near-antiques at **Hôtel Résidence Lord Byron (68)** (€-€€) (*5 rue Chateaubriand, 8th, 01-43.59.89.98, www.hotel-lord byron.fr*) lend a warm ambience while the courtyard soothes the senses. **Galileo Hôtel (69)** (€€) (*54 rue*

Galilée, 8th, 01-47.20.66.06, www.galileohotel.com) is elegant and sophisticated, modest and quiet. Luxurious yet minimalist, **L'Hôtel de Sers (34) (€€€€)** *(41 ave. Pierre 1er de Serbie, 8th, 01-53.23.75.75, www. hoteldesers.com)* was once a nobleman's *pied-à-terre*.

chapter 2

MADELEINE/OPÉRA

TUILERIES/LOUVRE/
PALAIS ROYAL

MADELEINE/OPÉRA TUILERIES/LOUVRE/ PALAIS ROYAL

Places to See:

1. Madeleine
2. OPÉRA GARNIER ★
4. Musée Gustave Moreau
27. Tuileries Gardens
28. Arc de Triomphe du Carrousel
29. LOUVRE MUSEUM ★
30. Louvre Pyramid
31. Place Vendôme
32. Palais Royal
33. Galerie Vivienne
34. Galerie Colbert
35. Place des Victoires
36. Jeu de Paume
37. Orangerie
38. Museum of Decorative Arts
39. Comédie Française
40. National Library-Richelieu Branch
41. Legrand Filles et Fils

Places to Eat & Drink:

3. Café de la Paix
5. Fauchon
6. Hédiard
7. Senderens
8. Farnesina
9. Ladurée
10. Cojean
11. Chez Jean
12. La Patata
13. Harry's New York Bar
42. L'Ardoise
43. Ferdi
44. Le Soufflé
45. Lescure
47. L'Écume St-Honoré
48. Le Pain Quotidien
49. Androüet Sur le Pouce
50. Le Carré des Feuillants
51. Angelina
52. Café Marly
53. Le Grand Véfour
54. L'Épi d'Or
55. Le Petit Flore
56. A Priori Thé
57. Chez Georges
58. Café Moderne
59. Aux Lyonnais
60. Bar Hemingway
61. Le Café des Initiés
62. Le Fumoir
63. Le Pulp

① **⑧** **⑫** *to Concorde;* **⑧** **⑫** **⑭** *to Madeleine;*
③ **⑦** **⑧** *to Opéra;* **⑦** **⑨** *to Chaussée d'Antin*

● SNAPSHOT ●

In the 19th century Baron Haussmann transformed Paris from a medieval fortress village into a modern city. With extraordinary vision he created wide, open boulevards that gave the city its aura of splendor and assured its place as one of the most beautiful cities of the world. Besides increasing ventilation and integrating the newly extended water and sewer systems, the avenues had the advantage of making it harder for rebellious citizens to erect barricades—a lesson learned from the revolutions which took place between 1789 and 1848. Nowhere is his extraordinary urban planning as visible as in the areas around Madeleine and the Opéra. The opulent use of space, in boulevards as well as buildings, has made it a prestigious location for the headquarters of major banks, while its bustling streets attract tourists, fashionistas, and people-watchers.

PLACES TO SEE
Landmarks:

North of the **Place de la Concorde** at the other end of rue Royale is the Neoclassical church known as **Madeleine (1)** *(pl. de la Madeleine, 8th, 01-44.51.69.00; hours: 9AM–7PM).* With its 52 Corinthian columns, it looks like a Greek temple. It faces what could be its mirror-image, the **National Assembly**, straight across Concorde and over the river. **Place de la Madeleine** is known for luxury food shops, but it was also home to luminaries: No. 9, for example, was Marcel Proust's childhood house. Follow the majestic Boulevard des Capucines, and you'll arrive at the ★ **OPÉRA GARNIER (2)** *(pl. de l'Opéra, 9th, 01-40.01.22.63, www.operadeparis.fr; box office hours: M–Sa 10:30AM–6:30PM)*. Tons of gilt and marble went into building the **Paris Opéra**. Its mix of styles, ranging from Classical to Baroque, features gold busts, winged angels, rearing horses, and ornate columns. The façade sculpture *La Danse* by Jean Baptiste Carpeaux was deemed so shockingly suggestive it was once splashed with ink. Inside, the auditorium has a false ceiling created by Marc Chagall in 1964. Named after its architect, Charles Garnier, the opera house is emblematic of Second Empire grandeur and excess. Garnier also built the sumptuous **Café de la Paix (3)** *(see also page 45)* on the corner of the Place de l'Opéra and Boulevard des Capucines.

TOP PICK!

Arts & Entertainment:

The **ballet company** of the **Opéra Garnier (2)** *(pl. de l'Opéra, 9th, 01-40.01.22.63, www.operadeparis.fr; box office hours: M–Sa 10:30AM–6:30PM)* performs classical and contemporary pieces. The Opéra also hosts modern dance companies from around the world. The wonderful **Musée Gustave Moreau (4)** *(14 rue de la Rochefoucauld, 9th, 01-48.74.38.50, www.musee-moreau.fr; hours: W–M 10AM–12:45PM, 2PM–5:15PM)* is devoted to this Symbolist painter's art, life, and obsessions.

PLACES TO EAT & DRINK
Where to Eat:

Place de la Madeleine is a cornucopia of restaurants and luxury groceries. **Fauchon (5)** (€€) *(24-26 pl. de la Madeleine, 8th, 01-70.39.38.00, reservations 01-70.39.38.39, www. fauchon.com; hours: café M–Sa*

9AM–10PM, deli M–Sa 8AM–9PM) is famous for its fabulous delicacies, as is **Hédiard (6)** (€€€) *(21 pl. de la Madeleine, 8th, 01-43.12.88.99, www.hediard.fr; hours: M–F 8:30AM–10PM, Sa 12PM–10:30PM)*; eat there or take it home. **Senderens (7)** (€€€-€€€€) *(9 pl. de la Madeleine, 8th, 01-42.65.22.90, www.lucascarton.com; hours: 12PM–2:45PM, 7:30PM–11:15PM, book ahead)*, in its Art Nouveau décor, serves divine dishes; the prix- fixe lunch will burn a smaller hole in your pocket. Isabelle Adjani and Inès de la Fressange swear by the fantastic Italian fare at **Farnesina (8)** (€€-€€€) *(9 rue Boissy d'Anglas, 8th, 01-42.66.65.57; hours: 12PM–2:30PM, 7:30PM–10:30PM)*. One of the most classic tearooms in Paris, **Ladurée (9)** (€-€€) *(16 rue Royale, 8th, 01-42.60.21.79, www.laduree.fr; hours: M–Sa 8:30AM–7PM, Su 10AM–7PM)* began as a bakery and sweet shop in 1862. Healthy soups, salads, and sandwiches at **Cojean (10)** (€) *(4-6 rue de Sèze, 9th, 01-40.06.08.80, www.cojean.fr; hours: M–F 8:30AM–6PM, Sa 9AM–7PM)* feature the freshest produce.

If you're at the Opéra, the **Café de la Paix (3)** (€€€-€€€€) *(Grand Hôtel Inter-Continental, 12 bd. des Capucines,*

9th, 01-40.07.36.36, www.cafedelapaix.fr; hours: 12PM–3PM, 6PM–11:30PM, terrace 9AM–11:30PM) is an experience, if not for a meal, then at least a *café express* and a sandwich on the terrace. The saying goes that if you sit there long enough, you'll see all the world go by. **Chez Jean (11) (€€)** *(8 rue St-Lazare, 9th, 01-48. 78.62.73; hours: M–F 12PM–2:30PM, 7:30PM–10:30PM, closed Aug)*, with the fresh seasonal creations of its capable chef, is a bargain for nouvelle cuisine. For a cheap eat, **La Patata (12) (€)** *(25 bd. des Italiens, 2nd, 01-42.68.16.66; hours: 11AM–12AM)* offers salads and baked potatoes with a variety of toppings.

Bars & Nightlife:

Café de la Paix (3) *(see also "Places to Eat & Drink", open to 1AM)*, is great for a relaxed people-watching evening. Ever classic, **Harry's New York Bar (13)** *(5 rue Daunou, 2nd, 01-42.61.71.14, www.harrys-bar.fr; hours: cocktail bar 10AM–4PM, piano bar M–Th 10PM–2PM, F–Sa 10PM–3PM)* is still popular with American ex-pats in Paris.

WHERE TO SHOP

Place de la Madeleine is known for luxury foodstuffs: **Fauchon (5)** and **Hédiard (6)** *(see also page 45)* are practically unbeatable. On the opposite side of the square, **Maille (14)** *(6 pl. de la Madeleine, 8th, 01-40.15.06.00)*, the famous mustard maker, sells divine mustards, vinegars, and olive oil. The specialty shop **Jadis et Gourmande (15)** *(27 rue Boissy d'Anglas, 8th, 01-42.65.23.23, www.jadisetgourmande.fr; hours: M 12PM–7PM, Tu–Sa 10AM–7PM)* is known for the *tresse*, a chocolate with nuts and candied orange peel. Or, to satisfy the craving for the perfect, small piece of oh-so-slightly bitter chocolate, head for La Maison du Chocolat (16) *(8 bd. de la Madeleine, 9th, 01-47.42.86.52, www.lamaisonduchocolat.com; hours: M–Sa 10AM–7:30PM)*. Treat yourself to some pampering at the beauty salon Institut Carita (18) *(11 rue du Faubourg-St-Honoré, 8th, 01-44.94.11.11, www.carita. fr)*. Eyeglasses have been the specialty of Lafont et Fils (19) *(11 rue Vignon, 8th, 01-47.42.25.93, www.lafont-paris.com; hours: M–Sa 10AM–7PM)* for three generations—conservative or eccentric, they make a fashion statement.

The **Place de l'Opéra** is encircled by specialty boutiques, like Lancel (20) *(8 pl. de l'Opera, 9th, 01-47.42.37.29, www.lancel.com; hours: M–F 10AM–7:30PM, Sa 10AM–8PM)* for leather goods and **Clerc** jewelers. Behind the Opéra on **Boulevard Haussmann** are two of Paris's most renowned department stores: Galeries Lafayette (21) *(40 bd. Haussmann, 9th, 01-42.82.34.56, www.galerieslafayette.com; hours: M–Sa 9:30AM–7:30PM, Th to 9PM)* and Au Printemps (22) *(64 bd. Haussmann, 9th, 01-42.82.50.00, Haussmann, 9th, 01-42.82.57.87, www.printemps.com; hours: M–Sa 9:35AM–7PM, Th to 10PM)*, which carry designer ready-to-wear, among other things. Several streets north, L'Atelier du Chocolat de Bayonne (23) *(107-109 rue St-Lazare, 9th, 01-40.16.09.13)* is famous for its chocolate bouquets. Adorn yourself with some jewelry from Cartier (25) *(13 rue de la Paix, 2nd, 01-58.18.23.00, www.cartier.com)*. Thierry Mugler (17) *(49 ave. de l'Opéra, 1st, 01-53.05.25.80, www.thierrymugler.com)* is a fashion boutique.

WHERE TO STAY

A feng shui expert helped design the Zen-inspired Golden Opéra de Noailles (24) (€€€) *(9 rue de la Michodière, 2nd, 01-47.42.92.90, US toll-free 800-344-1212, www.hotel denoailles.com)*. Luxury in a modern setting makes Park Hyatt Paris-Vendôme (26) (€€€€) *(5 rue de la Paix, 2nd, 01-58.71.12.34, www.paris.vendome.hyatt.com)* the destination for elegant but trendy travelers with deep pockets; the glass conservatory-dining room, with its potted orchids and displays of works by contemporary artists such as Ed Paschke and Llyn Foulkes, is especially pleasing.

TUILERIES/LOUVRE/ PALAIS ROYAL

1 **8** **12** *to Concorde;* **1** *to Tuileries, Palais Royal (Musée du Louvre), or Louvre/Rivoli;* **3** *to Bourse*

• SNAPSHOT •

The Louvre, the geographic center of Paris, was built as a fortress against the English in 1190. Around 1360 it was transformed into a royal residence, undergoing alterations by successive rulers over the centuries. In 1793 after the French Revolution it was turned into a museum with the royal collection on public display. It remains one of the major museums in the world, with a vast collection of art and antiquities. Stretching between the Louvre and Concorde, the Tuileries Gardens are an extension of the Louvre, with pavilions on either side housing other museums. Together with the opulent Place Vendôme and elegant Palais Royal to the north, this quarter affords a glimpse into the extravagant life of the French rulers and the power and riches of the *ancien régime*.

PLACES TO SEE
Landmarks:

Terraces, alleys, slopes, stairways, and stone pools were carefully planned for the royal **Tuileries Gardens (27)** *(rue de Rivoli/Quai François Mitterrand, 1st; hours: 7:30AM–7PM)* situated along the Seine on the eastern border of Concorde. Statues by 19th- and 20th-century artists complete the architectural whole with magnificent vistas in every direction. The **Arc de Triomphe du Carrousel (28)**—built to celebrate Napoleon's 1805 victories—stands between the Tuileries and the Louvre. Stand beneath the arch for a fantastic view of Paris, stretching in a straight line from the Louvre through the Tuileries, past Concorde, along the Champs-Elysées, through the Arc de Triomphe, across to the Grand Arch at La Défense, just beyond

TOP PICK!

Paris—an axis covering half the city. With nearly a third of a million works of art, the ★**LOUVRE MUSEUM (29)** *(rue de Rivoli, 1st, 01-40.20.51.51, www.louvre.fr; hours: Th, Sa–M 9AM–6PM, W, F 9AM–10PM)* boasts one of the greatest art collections in the world. Formerly a medieval fortress and Renaissance royal palace, the Louvre became a museum after the Revolution. Its treasures include masterpieces of Egyptian, Etruscan, Greek, Roman, and Oriental art, as well as more modern European works. Some of the most famous pieces are Leonardo da Vinci's *Mona Lisa*, the *Greek Winged Victory of Samothrace*, *Venus de Milo*, and the Assyrian *Winged Bull with Human Head*. A modern counterpoint to the museum's historic architectural splendor, I. M. Pei's striking 1989 glass **Louvre Pyramid (30)** *(courtyard)*, serves as the museum's main entrance.

The surrounding reflecting pools create a dizzying mirror image of the glass and steel structure while small pyramids echo the larger one's effect. The riverfront views are spectacular. Bordering the Tuileries and the Louvre to the north, **rue de Rivoli**, with its long row of arches, is home to expensive hotels, boutiques, and bookshops.

From rue de Rivoli, take rue de Castiglione and you'll arrive at one of Paris's most majestic squares, **Place Vendôme (31)** *(connecting to the Opéra via rue de la Paix)*. Built by Versailles architect Mansart, the octagonal square is an elegant example of harmonious, graceful 17th-century architecture. Many of the mansions were homes of bankers; one of them, No. 15, is now the **Hôtel Ritz (90)** *(see also page 59)*, where Coco Chanel lived, not far from her *salon de couture*. No. 12 was the house in which Chopin died in 1849. Today, under the arches encircling the square at ground level, **Place Vendôme (31)** is home to the haute jewelers of the world.

Just north of the Louvre is **Palais Royal (32)** *(pl. du Palais-Royal, 1st; hours: gardens 7:30AM–8:30PM)*, which has been through many phases—once Cardinal Richelieu's palace, then the childhood home of Louis XIV, and later the scene of elaborate and lavish gatherings as well as gambling and indulgent, rowdy celebrations. Today its arched courtyard bustles with boutiques and restaurants. Not to be missed are the stunning early 19th-century shopping arcades *(passages or galeries)*, with their high vaulted roofs of glass and iron. From the far (north) end of Palais Royal, take rue Vivienne then turn right onto rue des Petits Champs. To the left you'll find **Galerie Vivienne (33)** and **Galerie Colbert (34)**—

wander into any *galerie*, but be sure to check out these two. Rue des Petits Champs turns into La Feuillade before reaching the elegant fashion mecca, **Place des Victoires (35)** *(rue la Feuillade, 1st/2nd)*, built around a statue of Louis XIV.

Arts & Entertainment:

Museums abound: the **Louvre (29)** *(see also page 50)* for arts and antiquities, the **Jeu de Paume (36)** *(Jardin des Tuileries, pl. de la Concorde, 8th, 01-47.03.12.50, www.jeudepaume.org; hours: Tu 12PM–9PM, W–F 12PM–7PM, Sa–Su 10AM–7PM)* for contemporary art, the **Orangerie (37)** *(pl. de la Concorde, 1st, 01-44.77. 80.07, www.musee-orangerie.fr; hours: W–Th, Sa–M 12:30PM–7PM, F 12:30PM–9PM; groups W–M 9AM– 12:30PM)* for great Impressionist works, and the **Museum of Decorative Arts (38)** *(Palais de Louvre, 107 rue de Rivoli, 1st, 01-44.55.57.50, www.lesartsdecoratifs.fr; hours: Tu–W, F 11AM–6PM, Th 11AM–9PM, Sa–Su 10AM–6PM)* for art and design and its Art Nouveau and Art Deco collections. Near the Palais Royal entrance, France's finest classical theater is staged at the **Comédie Française (39)** *(2 rue de Richelieu, 1st, 08-25.10.16.80, www.comedie-francaise.fr; box office hours: M–Sa 11AM–6PM)*. The **National Library-Richelieu Branch (40)** *(58 rue de Richelieu, 2nd, 01-53.79.53.79, www.bnf.fr; hours: Tu–Sa 10AM–7PM, Su 12PM–7PM)*, north of Palais Royal, became an exhibition space once its books were moved to the Mitterand branch. For a change of pace, **Legrand Filles et Fils (41)** *(1 rue de la Banque, 2nd, 01- 42.60.07.12, www.caves-legrand.com; hours: M 11AM–*

7PM, Tu–F 10AM–7:30PM, Sa 10AM–7PM) offers wine courses focusing on a region or producer.

PLACES TO EAT & DRINK
Where to Eat:

The area bordered by Tuileries, Concorde, Place Vendôme, and Palais Royal is replete with cozy restaurants. Though Place Vendôme is one of the priciest spots in town, the nearby **L'Ardoise (42)** (€€) *(28 rue du Mont-Thabor, 1st, 01-42.96.28.18, www.lardoise-paris.com; hours: Tu–Sa 12PM–2:30PM, 6:30PM–11PM, Su 6:30PM–11PM)* is reasonably priced for good New Bistro fare. A few doors down, fashionistas feast on great burgers at lunch and tapas for dinner at **Ferdi (43)** (€€) *(32 rue du Mont-Thabor, 1st, 01-42.60.82.52; hours: Tu–Sa lunch & dinner)*; you might spot Penelope Cruz there. Two doors away, **Le Soufflé (44)** (€€) *(36 rue du Mont-Thabor, 1st, 01-42.60.27.19; hours: 12PM–2:30PM, 7PM–10PM, closed 3 wks Aug)*, an American favorite, offers a large variety of sweet and savory soufflés. Two streets down, quantity is the key word at **Lescure (45)** (€€) *(7 rue de Mondovi, 1st, 01-42.60.18.91; closed Su)*, where the tables are so close together you can rub shoulders with your neighbor.

At **L'Écume St-Honoré (47)** (€) *(6 rue du Marché-St-Honoré, 1st, 01-42.61.93.87; hours: Tu–F 8:30AM–2PM, 4PM–7:30PM, F until 10PM, Sa 8:30AM–10PM)*, you'll feel like you're in Brittany eating fresh oysters at a seaside shack. Communal wooden tables make brunch a rustic affair at **Le Pain Quotidien (48)** (€€) *(18 pl. du Marché-St-Honoré, 1st, 01-42.96.31.70; hours: 7AM–7PM, May 1–Oct 1 7AM–11PM)*. The cheese bar **Androuët Sur le Pouce (49)** (€) *(49 rue St-Roch, 1st, 01-42.97.57.39; hours: M–F 11:30AM–2:30PM, 7PM–9:30PM)* is great for lunch on the run and quiet dinners; it serves sand-

wiches, platters, and more. Splurge at **Le Carré des Feuillants (50)** (€€€€) *(14 rue de Castiglione, 1st, 01-42.86.82.82, www.carredesfeuillants.fr; hours: M–F 12PM– 2PM, 7:30PM–10PM)*, where the haute cuisine is fantastic and the service is superb. At least once, try the decadent desserts and rich hot chocolate at the old-world tea salon **Angelina (51)** (€) *(226 rue de Rivoli, 1st, 01-42.60.82.00; hours: M–F 9:30AM– 6:45PM, Sa–Su 9AM–7PM)*.

One goes to **Café Marly (52)** (€€) *(93 rue de Rivoli, 1st, 01-49.26.06.60; hours: 8AM–2AM)*, facing I.M. Pei's pyramid, for its amazing setting and to see and be seen. The famous **Le Grand Véfour (53)** (€€€€) *(17 rue de Beaujolais, 1st, 01-42.96.56.27, www.grand-vefour.com; hours: M–Th 12:30PM–1:30PM, 8PM–9:30PM, F 12:30PM–2PM, closed 1 wk Apr, during Aug, & Dec 24-31)*, bordering the gardens of Palais Royal, is one of the most beautiful restaurants of Paris. Mirrors reflect the Napoleonic splendor of elegant ceiling and wall paint-ings, sculpted cornices, and hanging light fixtures. It was frequented by Colette, Jean Cocteau, Victor Hugo, and Napoleon. To avoid paying an arm and a leg, try the prix-fixe lunch. For good value and a brasserie that seems like it hasn't changed in decades, **L'Épi d'Or (54)** (€-€€) *(25 rue Jean-Jacques Rousseau, 1st, 01-42. 36.38.12; hours: open to 11PM, closed Sa lunch, Su, & Aug)* has "French" stamped all over it; best to reserve for dinner and be on time. Great quality, inexpensive prices, and traditional cuisine make **Le Petit Flore (55)** (€) *(6 rue Croix des Petits Champs, 1st, 01-42.60.25.53)* hard to beat, but it's open for lunch only.

In the lavish **Galerie Vivienne (33)** near **Place des Victoires (35)** *(see also page 52)*, an indoor terrace with glass arcade gives warmth to the upscale tea salon **A Priori Thé (56)** (€€) *(35-37 Galerie Vivienne, 2nd, 01-42.97.48.75; hours: M–F 9AM–6PM, Sa 9AM–6:30PM, Su 12PM–6:30PM)*; it also serves weekend brunch. On the other side of **Place des Victoires (35)**, the trendy crowd flocks to the famous Parisian bistro **Chez Georges (57)** (€€€) *(1 rue du Mail, 2nd, 01-42.60.07.11; hours: M–F 12PM–2PM, 7PM–10PM, closed Aug)* for an authentic experience of classic French food. Further north, across from the Bourse (old stock market), **Café Moderne (58)** (€€) *(40 rue Notre-Dame-des-Victoires, 2nd, 01-53.40.84.10, www.cafemoderne.fr; hours: M–F breakfast, lunch, dinner; Sa dinner only)*—stylish, chic, yet cozy—boasts an eclectic menu with international flavors. Nearby, the draw at **Aux Lyonnais (59)** (€€-€€€) *(32 rue St-Marc, 2nd, 01-42.96.65.04, www.alain-ducasse.com; hours: Tu–F 12PM–2PM, 7:30PM–11PM, Sa 7:30PM–11PM)*, besides vintage bistro décor, is its owner, Alain Ducasse; the prices are very reasonable for Lyonnais cooking from this celebrated chef.

Bars & Nightlife:

Bar Hemingway (60) *(Hôtel Ritz, 15 pl. Vendôme, 1st, 01-43.16.33.65, www.ritzparis.com; hours: M–Sa 6:30PM–2AM, Su 11AM–5PM)*, made famous by its most illustrious client Papa H, might be a cliché but the wood and leather luxury exudes charm. **Le Café des Initiés (61)** *(3 pl. des Deux-Ecus, 1st, 01-42.33.78.29; hours: M–Sa 7:30AM– 1AM)* is a trendy *apéritif* hangout with friendly staff. For more elegance and a slightly colonial air, try **Le Fumoir (62)** *(6 rue de l'Amiral-de-Coligny, 1st, 01-42.92.00.24, www.lefumoir.com; hours: 11AM–2PM)*. Although **Le Pulp (63)** *(25 bd. Poissonnière, 2nd, 01-40.26.01.93, www.pulp-paris.com; call for hours)* is an enormously popular and trendy lesbian club. It draws a mixed crowd on free nights: Wednesday and Thursday.

WHERE TO SHOP

Walk through the arches of the rue de Rivoli, where boutiques and bookstores will catch your eye, including WH Smith (64) *(248 rue de Rivoli, 1st, 01-44.77.88.99, www.whsmith.fr)*, the renowned English bookseller. Across the rue de Rivoli from the Louvre, the Louvre des Antiquaires (65) *(2 pl. du Palais-Royal, 1st, 01-42.97.27.27, www.louvre-antiquaires.com)* houses 250 reputable dealers of high-quality antiques.

Fine jewels are the theme at **Place Vendôme (31)** *(see also page 51)*, where the great names of jewelry design sparkle with their gems: among them, Mauboussin (66) *(20 pl. Vendôme, 1st, 01-44.55.10.10, www.mauboussin.com)*, Van Cleef & Arpels (67) *(22 pl. Vendôme, 1st, 01-*

53.45.35.50, www.vancleef-arpels. com), **Boucheron (68)** (26 pl. Vendôme, 1st, 01-42.61.58.16, www.boucheron.com), and **Chanel (69)** (18 pl. Vendôme, 1st, 01-55.35.50.05, www.chanel.com). For gems of another sort, take a whiff of jewelry designer Joel Rosenthal's exclusive perfumes at **JAR (72)** (14 rue de Castiglione, 1st, 01-40.20. 47.20). At

the same address, sexy stilettos by **Rodolphe Ménudier (73)** (14 rue de Castiglione, 1st, 01-42.60.86.27) are sure to turn heads. For classic men's shirts and pajamas, **Charvet (74)** (28 pl. Vendôme, 1st, 01-42.60.30.70) has been shirt-maker to royalty and bourgeoisie since 1838.

Rue St-Honoré, just south of **Place Vendôme (31)** (see also page 51), is one of the most famous shopping streets of Paris. To the west it's called rue du Faubourg-St-Honoré. As you walk eastward the shops go from extremely expensive couturiers to more moderate designer boutiques to the humbler shops of Les Halles. A few blocks east of Place Vendôme is an original Paris concept store, **Colette (75)** (213 rue St-Honoré, 1st, 01-55.35.33.90, www.colette.fr; hours: M–Sa 11am–7pm), a design emporium of clothing, art objects, and electronics, with a photo gallery, bookshop, and exhibition space. **Jacques Le Corre (76)** (193 rue St-Honoré, 1st, 01-42.96.97.40, www.jacqueslecorre.com) designs stylish but practical hats, bags, and shoes.

In the Palais Royal courtyard be sure to visit Italian costume jewelry designer **Donatella Pellini (77)** (20 gal.

de Montpensier, Jardins du Palais Royal, 1st, 01-42.96. 18.68), whose whimsical, elegant designs use stones and resins in cascades of colors and intriguing shapes. The destination for vintage haute couture is Didier Ludot (78) *(20-24 gal. de Montpensier, Jardins du Palais Royal, 1st, 01-42.96.06.56, www.didierludot.com)*. Alongside the Palais Royal, Martin Margiela (79) *(25 bis, rue de Montpensier, 1st, 01-40.15.07.55)*, protégé of Jean Paul Gaultier, has opened his own boutique of inventive clothing and accessories. At **Galerie Vivienne (33)** *(see also page 51)* you'll find stylish boutiques, such as Jean Paul Gaultier (80) *(No. 6, Galerie Vivienne, 1st, 01-42.86.05.05, www.jeanpaulgaultier.com)*. Christian Astuguevieille (81) *(No. 42, Galerie Vivienne, 2nd, 01-44.69.91.40; hours: by appt only)* showcases furniture designs, sculpture, and drawings. Galerie Véro-Dodat (82) *(rue du Bouloi/Jean-Jacques Rousseau, 1st)* is another *passage* of antiquaries, vintage shops, and furniture designers.

Place des Victoires (35) *(see also page 52)* is the locus of major fashion boutiques, including Kenzo (84) *(3 pl. des Victoires, 1st, 01-40.39.72.03, www.kenzo. com)*. You'll find that the apparel and accessory wonders at Lucien Pellat-Finet (85) *(2 rue d'Aboukir, 2nd, 01-53.00.98.00, www.lucienpellat-finet.com)* are perfectly suited to the store's décor. A street away, Sandrine Philippe (86) *(6 rue Hérold, 1st, 01-40.26. 21.78)* designs sophisticated, romantic fashions with a way of making you feel like you're part of a story behind her clothes. Next door you'll find luxurious fabrics rich in color and texture at **Dominique Kieffer (87)** *(8 rue Hérold, 1st, 01-42.21.32.44, www.dominiquekieffer.com)*, who creates textiles with soul.

WHERE TO STAY

Clean and comfortable, **Hôtel Vivienne (70)** (€) *(40 rue Vivienne, 2nd, 01-42.33.13.26)* is a good budget hotel. The best rooms at **Hôtel Brighton (88)** (€€-€€€) *(218 rue de Rivoli, 1st, 01-47.03.61.61, www.esprit-de-france. com)* have great views. Overlooking the Tuileries Gardens, the very expensive **Hôtel Meurice (89)** (€€€€) *(228 rue de Rivoli, 1st, 01-44.58.10.10, www.hotel meurice.com)* boasts a discerning clientele—including actor Rupert Everett—and its spa is divine. Pure, unabashed luxury reigns at the **Hôtel Ritz (90)** (€€€€) *(15 pl. Vendôme, 1st, 01-43.16.30.70/71/72, www.ritzparis. com)*. If you don't like flamboyance, **Hôtel Costes (91)** (€€€€) *(239 rue St-Honoré, 1st, 01-42.44.50.00, www.hotelcostes.com)* isn't for you. More intimate, with painted beams and picturesque furnishings, is **Le Relais St-Honoré (92)** (€€-€€€) *(308 rue St-Honoré, 1st, 01-42.96.06.06, www.relaissainthonore.com)*—you might think you've been transported to a charming country manor. And within walking distance from Palais Royal, **Hôtel Thérèse (93)** (€€-€€€) *(5-7 rue Thérèse, 1st, 01-42.96.10.01, www.hoteltherese.com)* offers subdued luxury.

chapter 3

LES HALLES/ MONTORGUEIL

HÔTEL DE VILLE/ BEAUBOURG

MARAIS

LES HALLES/MONTORGUEIL HÔTEL DE VILLE/BEAUBOURG MARAIS

Places to See:

1. Forum des Halles
2. Halles Garden
3. Fontaine des Innocents
4. Pavillon des Arts
5. St-Eustache
6. Bourse de Commerce
7. Tour Jean Sans Peur
8. Théâtre du Châtelet
49. Place du Châtelet
50. Théâtre de la Ville
51. Tour St-Jacques
52. Hôtel de Ville
53. St. Gervais-St. Protais
54. Cloître des Billettes
55. St-Merri
56. CENTRE GEORGES POMPIDOU ★
57. Fontaine de Stravinsky
58. Rue Quincampoix
59. 51 rue de Montmorency
60. IRCAM
61. Musée de la Poupée
62. Musée d'Art et d'Histoire du Judaïsme
63. L'Atelier de Fred
64. Musée des Arts et Métiers
84. Hôtel de Sens

85. Shoah Memorial
87. Hôtel de Sully
88. Place des Vosges
89. Victor Hugo House
90. Musée Carnavalet
91. Musée Cognacq-Jay
92. Picasso Museum
93. Hôtel de Rohan
94. Hôtel de Soubise
95. Rue Vieille-du-Temple
96. Rue Ste-Croix-de-la-Bretonnerie
97. Museum of Magic
98. Maison Européenne de la Photographie
99. La Galerie d'Architecture

Places to Eat & Drink:

9. Au Pied de Cochon
10. Restaurant Chez Max
11. Chez Denise—La Tour de Montlhéry
12. Le Père Fouettard
13. Au Chien qui Fume
14. Le Louchebem
15. La Victoire Suprème du Coeur
16. L'Ostréa

★ **Top Picks**

Where to Stay:

LES HALLES/MONTORGUEIL

④ to Les Halles; ① ④ ⑦ ⑪ ⑭ to Châtelet;
⑦ to Pont Neuf; ① to Louvre-Rivoli;
④ to Étienne Marcel;
③ to Sentier; ③ ④ to Réaumur-Sébastopol;
④ ⑧ ⑨ to Strasbourg-St-Denis

● SNAPSHOT ●

Les Halles was once the farmers' market of Paris, sheltered beneath beautiful glass and cast-iron pavilions. When Émile Zola dubbed it "the belly of Paris," he was referring to the food market, but the description applied equally to the unsavory and "alternate" characters who inhabited the area. The pavilions were demolished in 1969 and were later replaced by the Forum des Halles, an underground mall and transportation hub. A mixed mass of humanity still crowds the streets, and rue St-Denis has long been a red-light district, but there are plenty of remarkable spots in Les Halles. More picturesque, however, is the hip Montorgueil area, directly north of the Forum. The small streets around rue Tiquetonne and rue Étienne Marcel turn up funky

 corners and trendy finds. All-night bistros thrive in Les Halles, while Montorgueil is crammed with romantic cafés as well as food and wine merchants slightly reminiscent of the old Halles.

PLACES TO SEE
Landmarks:

The **Forum des Halles (1)** *(rues Rambuteau/Pierre Lescot/Berger, 1st)* is a three-level mall with shops, cinemas, and a pool. Despite its open central courtyard, it's rather gloomy. The surrounding landscape, the **Halles Garden (2)** *(west of Forum des Halles, 1st)*, is as devoid of charm as the Forum. Architecture and city planning buffs are challenged by this bad 1970s attempt at urban renewal. Kitty-cornered (SE) from the Forum is the **Fontaine des Innocents (3)** *(rue Berger/rue Pierre Lescot, 1st)*, a Renaissance fountain erected on the site of the Innocents Cemetery, from which vast numbers of corpses were moved in 1785 to the Catacombs *(see Chapter 6, page 147)*. In the diametrically opposite corner of the Forum is a mushroom-shaped glass-and-steel structure, the **Pavillon des Arts (4)** *(101 rue Rambuteau, 1st, 01-42.33.82.50; call for shows)*, an exhibition space.

Among this mishmash of futuristic bad taste is one of Paris's most magnificent churches, **St-Eustache (5)** *(rue du Jour, 1st, 01-42.36.31.05, www.st-eustache.org; hours: M–F 9:30AM–7PM, Sa 10AM–7PM, Su 9:15AM–7PM)*, north of the **Halles Garden (2)** *(see also above)*. Modeled on Notre-Dame, with its flying buttresses, its plan is Gothic, but the decoration is sumptuously Renaissance. Historic figures are affiliated with this church, where Cardinal Richelieu and the Marquise de Pompadour (Louis XV's official mistress) were baptized. Another interesting building is nearby: at the east end of the **Halles Garden (2)**, the **Bourse de Commerce (6)**

(2 rue de Viarmes, 1st, 01-42.21.30.50; hours: by appt M–F 9AM–6PM) provides group tours of this commodities market.

St-Eustache (5) *(see also page 65)* marks the beginning of a more soulful area north of Les Halles. Stroll along the narrow **rue Montorgueil** and take in the flavors of the fruit and vegetable vendors, the wine and cheese merchants, and the ubiquitous cafés. The **Tour Jean Sans Peur (7)** *(20 rue Étienne Marcel, 2nd, 01-40.26.20.28, www.tourjeansanspeur.com; hours: Apr–Nov W–Su 1:30PM–6PM, Nov–Mar W, Sa–Su 1:30PM–6PM)* was the Duke of Burgundy's attempt to protect himself from reprisals after he assassinated his rival, the Duke of Orleans, which was believed to have ignited the 100 Years' War. Burgundian symbols—oak, hawthorn, and hops—are carved into the turret. Rues Montorgueil, Tiquetonne, and Étienne Marcel are fun, funky places to explore around the Forum and are a bit more appealing to the eyes.

Arts & Entertainment:

The **Pavillon des Arts (4)** *(see also page 65)* exhibits unusual works, often showcasing unique objects or themes, from French as well as foreign museums. The free recitals at **St-Eustache (5)** *(Su 5:30PM), (see also page 65)* feature its 8,000-pipe organ. **Théâtre du Châtelet (8)** *(1 pl. du Châtelet, 1st, west side of the square, info 01-40.28.28.00, booking 01-40.28.28.41, www.chatelet-theatre.com)* is one of Paris's main venues for classical music, opera, and dance; its annual *Bleu sur Scène* blues festival brings major artists, like Herbie Hancock and Ornette Coleman.

PLACES TO EAT & DRINK
Where to Eat:

Though fast-food joints glut Les Halles, you can still eat well at a number of restaurants and cafés. A stone's throw from the **Bourse de Commerce (6)** *(see also pages 65-66)* is a brasserie once frequented by market workers: **Au Pied de Cochon (9)** (€€-€€€) *(6 rue Coquillière, 1st, 01-40. 13.77.00, www.pieddecochon.com; hours: open 24/7)* serves such classics as onion soup and oysters, but its specialty is grilled pig's feet in béarnaise sauce. You won't leave **Restaurant Chez Max (10)** (€) *(47 rue St-Honoré, 1st, 01-45.08.80.13, www.chezmax.fr; hours: Tu–Sa 12PM– 2PM, 7:30PM–11PM)* hungry—with its three-course meals, including a carafe of red or white wine—this is a great bargain. Several restaurants just south of Halles offer good deals. Fun, friendly, and open all night, **Chez Denise—La Tour de Montlhéry (11)** (€€-€€€) *(5 rue des Prouvaires, 1st, 01-42.36.21.82; hours: 12PM–3PM, 7:30PM–5:30AM)* serves excellent classics and is frequented by artists, writers, and professional business "suits" alike. Inexpensive and relaxing, **Le Père Fouettard (12)** (€) *(9 rue Pierre Lescot, 1st, 01-42.33.74.17; hours: 7:30AM–2AM)* has a year-round terrace. **Au Chien qui Fume (13)** (€€) *(33 rue du Pont-Neuf, 1st, 01-42.36.07.42, www.au-chien-qui-fume.com; hours: 12PM–2AM)* serves delicious brasserie classics, including braised rabbit; the décor's motif is dogs dressed as people—the place is, after all, "The Smoking Dog." **Le Louchebem (14)** (€-€€) *(31*

rue Berger, 1st, 01-42.33.12.99, www.le-louchebem.fr; hours: M–Sa open to 11:30PM) is a steak lover's haven and another Halles original. Excellent fresh fish is the specialty at **L'Ostréa (16)** (€€-€€€) *(4 rue Sauval, 1st, 01-40.26.08.07; hours: M–F 12PM–2PM, 7:30PM–10:30PM, Sa 7:30PM–10:30PM).*

In the Montorgueil area, **La Potée des Halles (17)** (€–€€) *(3 rue Étienne Marcel, 1st, 01-40.41.98.15; hours: M, W–F 12PM–2:30PM, 7PM–11:30PM, Tu 12PM–2:30PM, Sa–Su 7PM–11:30PM, closed Aug)* is steamy with beans, cabbage, pork, and veal. Classified a national monument, its tiled walls depict hand-painted beer and coffee goddesses. The original chairs display the names of Halles workers who were regulars; some of them still are, at 70 or 80. Another authentic working-class haunt, **Le Cochon à l'Oreille (18)** (€) *(15 rue Montmartre, 1st, 01-42.36.07.56; hours: M–Sa 12PM–3PM, 6PM–1AM)* serves huge, hearty portions to a mostly French clientele. In the lively food market street, rue Montorgueil, from which the area gets its name, **Foody's Brunch Café (19)** (€) *(26 rue Montorgueil, 1st, 01-40.13.02.53; hours: M–Sa 11:30AM–5PM, closed first 3 wks Aug)* is a self-service vegetarian restaurant with soups, salads, fresh juice, and bakery goods at great prices. Artistry and imagination are bywords at gay restaurant **Aux Trois Petits Cochons (20)** (€€) *(31 rue Tiquetonne, 2nd, 01-42.33.39.69, www.auxtrois petitscochons.fr, dinner only),* where the food is noteworthy and the presentation carefully arranged. The owners' success led to a second restaurant a street away: more informal, **Pig'z (21)** (€€) *(5 rue Marie Stuart, 2nd, 01-42.33.05.89, www.pigz.fr, dinner only; hours: Tu–Sa open from 8PM)* is just as popular, so reserve a table. You'll get a shot of local neighbors and artists at both places. The oldest *pâtisserie* in Paris, classified as a historical monument, **Stohrer (22)** (€) *(51 rue Montorgueil, 2nd, 01-42.33.38.20, www.stohrer.fr; hours: 7:30AM–8:30PM)* was opened in 1730 by Marie Antoinette's personal baker. Now we know why she said, "Let them eat cake!" Around the corner, at the classic, old-style bistro **Aux Crus de Bourgogne (23)** (€€) *(3 rue Bachaumont, 2nd, 01-42.33.48.24; hours: open to 11PM)* nostalgia is served up with the house specialty, fresh lobster. **La Crêpe Dentelle (30)** (€) *(10 rue Léopold Bellan, 2nd, 01-40.41.04.23; hours: M–F 11:30AM–3:30PM, 7:30PM–11PM, Sa 7:30PM–11PM)* is a family-run *crêperie* serving an array of delicious crêpes and indulgent desserts.

Bars & Nightlife:

Kong (24) *(1 rue du Pont-Neuf, 1st, 01-40.39.09.00, www.kong.fr; hours: happy hour 6PM–8PM, music bar 10:30PM–2AM, restaurant 10:30AM–2AM)* is one of the city's hot spots designed by hotshot Philippe Starck and featured on *Sex and the City*—the too-too-cool staff is part of the heavy-on-style, light-on-substance ambience. One of the most famous jazz clubs in Europe is **Le Slow Club (25)** *(130 rue de Rivoli, 1st, 01-42.33.84.30; call for*

for hours), with big band and R&B rocking the tiny space. **Rue des Lombards** in Les Halles is known for live jazz. Among the notable clubs of the street are **Au Duc des Lombards (26)** *(42 rue des Lombards, 1st, 01-42.33.22.88, www.ducdeslombards.com; hours: M–Sa, call for hours)*, and **Baiser Salé (27)** *(58 rue des Lombards, 1st, 01-42.33.37.71)*. Included in the list is also **Le Sunset/Le Sunside (28)** *(60 rue des Lombards, 1st, 01-40.26.21.25/01-40.26.46.60, www.sunset-sunside.com; call for hours)*, where artists from both sides of the Atlantic play (electric in the former; acoustic, the latter). Lively **Bistrot d'Eustache (29)** *(€-€€)* *(37 rue Berger, 1st, 01-40.26.23.20; call for hours)*, a charming throwback to the jazz age of the 1930s and 1940s, serves traditional French food; the jazz is live, with gypsy guitar jazz on Thursday nights.

WHERE TO SHOP

La Grande Boutique de l'Artisan Parfumeur (31) *(2 rue l'Amiral Coligny, 1st, 01-44.88.27.50, www.laboutique delartisanparfumeur.com)* is the flagship store of the grand perfume specialist. Besides selling fragrances, candles, and creams, the place gives evening lectures on the art and history of perfumery. With clothing by up-and-coming avant-garde designers, graffiti-filled walls, and photo exhibits, **Surface to Air Boutique (32)** *(46 rue l'Arbre Sec, 1st, 01-49.27.04.54, www.surface2air.com)* is the cat's meow in concept stores. If you must take home an enamel Parisian street sign, go to **Plaques et Pots (33)** *(12 rue de la Ferronnerie, 1st, 01-42.36. 21.72)*.

Hop to the other side of Les Halles for all manner of kitchen utensils and tableware at the famous **E. Dehillerin (34)** *(18 rue Coquillière, 1st, 01-42.36.53.13, www. e-dehillerin.fr; hours: M 9AM–12:30PM, 2PM–6PM, Tu–Sa 9AM–6PM)*. The competition is equally famous: **A. Simon (35)** *(48 rue Montmartre, 2nd, 01-42.33.71.65, www.a-simon.fr)* and **Mora (36)** *(13 rue Montmartre, 1st, 01-45.08.19.24, www.mora.fr; hours: M–F 9AM–6:15PM, Sa 9:30AM–1PM, 1:45PM–6PM)*. For all manner of beads, ribbon, buttons, yarn, and trim, visit **La Droguerie (37)** *(9-11 rue du Jour, 1st, 01-45.08.93.27, www.ladroguerie. com; hours: M 2PM–6:45PM, Tu–Sa 10:30AM–6:45PM)*. Rue du Jour has spawned a small **Agnès b (38)** *(2, 3, 6, 19 rue du Jour, 1st, women 01-45.08.56.56, men 01-*

42.33.04.13, children 01-40.39. 96.88, infants 01-42.33.27.34, www.agnesb.com) empire, where black is the staple wardrobe color and some bright patterns are mixed in for fun. For the little black beret, little black suit, little black cardigan, head to Claudie Pierlot (39) *(1 rue Montmartre, 1st, 01-42.21.38.38, www.claudiepierlot.com)*.

When the walking gets to you, enter the medieval stone walls of Spa Nuxe (40) *(32 rue Montorgueil, 1st, 01-55.80.71.40, www.nuxe.com)* for an exotic serene experience of their treatments, or just pick up a few beauty products. Conversely, try the hammam (Turkish bath) at Aux Bains Montorgueil (41) *(55 rue Montorgueil, 2nd, 01-44.88.01.78)* for a steam bath, an exfoliation, and a massage.

If sewing and crafts are your passion, don't miss Declercq Passementiers (42) *(15 rue Étienne Marcel, 1st, 01-44.76.90.70, www.declercqpassementiers.fr)* for fantastic trimmings and tassels. Walk along the trendy **rue Étienne Marcel**, lined with hip names in fashion—Yohji Yamamoto, Joseph, and Diesel, among others. In the Montorgueil quarter, **rue Tiquetonne** is a trendsetter. It's full of workshops, restaurants, and boutiques, including Killiwatch (43) *(64 rue Tiquetonne, 2nd, 01-42.21.17.37)*, a designer and secondhand clothing store. Increasingly popular, it sells used fashions by the kilo. Next door, the elegant, sexy, and feminine shoes at Patrick Cox **(44)** *(62 rue Tiquetonne, 2nd, 01-40. 26.66.55)* practically strut off the catwalk. One street up, between rue St-Denis and rue Dussoubs, is the Passage du Grand Cerf **(45)** *(St-Denis/rue Dussoubs, www.passagedugrandcerf.com)*, with its Belle Époque ironwork and funky, fashionable purveyors of clothing, accessories, lighting, and art objects; prominent shops include **As'Art** *(No. 3)*, for unique African and ethnic gifts, **MX Sylvie Branellec** *(No. 6)*, with jewelry focused on pearls, and **PM CO Style** *(No. 5)*, for a variety of fasci-nating design objects from the far corners of Earth. Barbara Bui **(46)** *(23 rue Etienne Marcel, 2nd, 01-40.26.43.65, www.barbarabui.com)* reflects her French and Vietnamese roots with refined and graceful design-er clothes. Gourmet cookbooks, old and new, abound at Librairie Gourmande **(86)** *(90 rue Montmartre, 2nd, 01-43.54.37.27, www.librairie-gourmande.fr; hours: M–Sa 11AM–7PM):* they include French, American, and English editions.

WHERE TO STAY

Les Halles isn't the best place to stay, but the Montorgueil area affords some bargains. Ambience is missing at the **Tiquetonne Hotel (47)** (€) *(6 rue Tiquetonne, 2nd, 01-42.36.94.58),* but it's cheap, clean, and very, very basic (with chenille bedspreads). **Hôtel du Cygne (48)** (€-€€) *(3 rue du Cygne, 1st, 01-42.60.14.16, www.hotelducygne.fr)* is reliable, appealing, and livable, with rooms decorated in Laura Ashley style.

HÔTEL DE VILLE/BEAUBOURG

① ④ ⑦ ⑪ ⑭ *to Châtelet;*
① ⑪ *to Hôtel de Ville;* ⑪ *to Rambuteau;*
③ ⑪ *to Arts et Métiers;*
③ ④ *to Réaumur-Sébastopol;*
④ ⑧ ⑨ *to Strasbourg-St-Denis*

● **SNAPSHOT** ●

Dominated by the Hôtel de Ville (town hall) and the Centre Georges Pompidou (colloquially referred to as "Beaubourg"), this district is jam-packed with interesting landmarks, museums, bars, and shops. Two aesthetics coexist: the ornate marble—replete with turrets and statues—of the Hôtel de Ville corresponds to the pomp and circumstance of its stature; a few streets away the "inside-out" structure of Beaubourg—with color-coded pipes, scaffolding, and ducts—puts the functional works of the building on public display. The district is exciting and vibrant, attracting a crowd eager for street spectacles —and there are plenty of those in the Hôtel de Ville/ Beaubourg quarter.

PLACES TO SEE
Landmarks:

Start at **Place du Châtelet (49)** *(at bd. De Sébastopol, 4th)*, which was once a fortress defending the city from the north and is now a major métro hub. Aboveground, in the center of the square, is a fountain—yet another monument to Napoleon's victories. On either side of

Place du Châtelet (49) are the twin theaters Théâtre du Châtelet (8) *(west side; see page 66)* and Théâtre de la Ville (50) *(east side; 2 pl. du Châtelet, 4th, 01-42.74.22.77, www.theatredelaville-paris.com)*. In the northeast corner, the Tour St-Jacques (51) *(Sq. de la Tour St-Jacques, 4th)* seems to oversee the area. Flamboyantly Gothic, the tower is what is left standing of a church that served as the meeting point for pilgrims before venturing out on voyages. The tower was a favorite of the Surrealists, perhaps because of the plethora of gargoyles or because of their incongruity with the figure at the base of the tower, a statue of Blaise Pascal, who conducted barometrical experiments at the site in the 17th century.

As you walk along the *quai* (embankment) of the Seine eastward, gaze along the river at the fabulous views. Across the Seine, you'll see the old Conciergerie prison *(see Chapter 5, page 125)*; further to the left, the cathedral of Notre-Dame *(see Chapter 5, page 126)*; and in the distance to the right, the Eiffel Tower *(see Chapter 1, page 24)*. Great photo ops! Continuing along the *quai*, you'll arrive at the Hôtel de Ville (52) *(pl. de l'Hôtel de Ville, 29 rue de Rivoli, 4th, 01-42.76.43.43)*, which serves as town hall, city council premises, and official residence of the mayor of Paris. It is also the venue for receptions honoring foreign dignitaries. With its elaborate, sculpted exterior and the impressive interior adorned with chandeliers, statues, caryatids, and a majestic staircase, the Hôtel de Ville (52) exudes power, pomp, and ceremony. The square facing the building has had its share of power-filled days: it was once the main site for public executions.

East of the **Hôtel de Ville (52)** is the 6th-century church **St. Gervais-St. Protais (53)** *(pl. St-Gervais, 4th, 01.48.87.32. 02; hours: M–F 6AM–9PM, Sa–Su 7AM–9PM)*, the façade of which is made up of three levels of columns—Doric, Ionic, and Corinthian. This beautiful

church is famous for its lovely religious music. Walk around the back, up the picturesque **rue des Barres** where artists set up their easels and small cafés cover the terraced sidewalk with tables and chairs. A few streets northwestward is the 7th-century church of **St-Merri (55)** *(76 rue de la Verrerie, 4th, 01-42.71.93.93; hours: 3PM–5PM)*, decidedly Gothic.

Follow the rue St-Martin two streets north and you'll come to the **★CENTRE GEORGES POMPIDOU (56)**, or "Beaubourg" *(pl. Georges Pompidou/rue Beaubourg, 4th, 01-44.78.12.33, www.centrepompidou.fr; hours: W–M 11AM–10PM).*

TOP PICK!

Opened in 1977, it was an immediate success and has remained so; its inside-out structure makes it one of the most unique examples of modern architecture. The workings of the building—air ducts, water shafts, utility pipes, elevators, escalators, and structural steel struts— are all on the outside, color-coded to distinguish their functions, while the glass and steel walls give a sense of interior-exterior permeability. This leaves the entire interior space with the flexibility to adapt to the center's activities and needs. The museum boasts a collection of more than 50,000 works, covering painting, sculpture, drawing, photography, architecture, design, cinema, video, and audiovisual archives in addition to a library, screening rooms, and performance and exhibition spaces.

Outside Beaubourg, on the large esplanade, pavement artists and street performers do their thing to crowds of willing onlookers. South of Beaubourg, the **Fontaine de Stravinsky (57)** *(pl. Igor Stravinsky, rue Brismiche, 4th)*, created by artists Niki de St-Phalle and Jean Tinguély, is an intermingling orchestra of delightfully colorful and fanciful creature sculptures, each contributing to the waterworks extravaganza. Along **rue Quincampoix (58)** *(rue des Lombards/rue Rambuteau, 4th)*, a bevy of galleries, cafés, and bars animate the cobblestone street and its restored 18th-century residences. A block past its northern end is the (probably) oldest house in Paris: **51 rue de Montmorency (59)** *(rue Beaubourg/rue St-Martin, 3rd; closed to public)* built in 1407.

Arts & Entertainment:

Théâtre de la Ville (50) *(see also page 76)* is a must-stop for modern dance fans, where many important choreographers, such as Maguy Marin and Jean-Claude Gallotta, have showcased their talents. The modern art exhibits, audiovisual screenings, and performance art at **Centre Georges Pompidou (56)** *(see also page 77)* are not to be missed. By the southern flank of Centre Pompidou, **IRCAM (60)** *(1 pl. Igor* *Stravinsky, 4th, 01-44.78.48.43, www.ircam.fr; call for show hours)*, dedicated to musical experimentation and research, offers contemporary music concerts; Pierre Boulez has been actively involved in IRCAM since its conception. A street north of Beaubourg, the **Musée de la Poupée (61)** *(impasse Berthaud, 3rd, 01-42.72.73.11, www.museedelapoupee paris.com; hours: Tu–Su 10AM–6PM)* exhibits dolls from around the world, has a doll hospital, and offers doll-making classes for adults and children. The **Musée d'Art et d'Histoire du Judaïsme (62)** *(Hôtel de St-Aignan, 71 rue du Temple, 3rd, 01-53.01.86.60, www.mahj.org; hours: M–F 11AM–6PM, Su 10AM–6PM)* is dedicated to French Jewish culture from the Middle Ages to the present. Take cooking classes (small groups) at **L'Atelier de Fred (63)** *(6 rue des Vertus, 3rd, 01-40.29.46.04, www.latelierdefred.com)* to impress your friends back home with an authentic, homemade Parisian meal. The **Musée des Arts et Métiers (64)** (Museum of Science and Industry) *(60 rue Réaumur, 3rd, 01-53.01.82.00, www.arts-et-metiers.net; hours: Tu–W, F–Su 10AM–6PM, Th 10AM–9:30PM)* hosts conferences ranging from Walkman technology to how to anticipate natural disasters; among other inventive objects, the mechanical figures and prototype machines are amusing.

PLACES TO EAT & DRINK
Where to Eat:

Take in the sights, from the fashion-model wait staff to the Parisian rooftops and major gems of the city, at **Georges (67)** (€€€) *(Centre Pompidou, 19 rue Beaubourg, 4th, 01-44.78.47.99; hours: W–M 11AM–2AM)*, the ultra-chic café-restaurant on the terrace of Beaubourg; the food's good and the view is superlative. Best for drinks, light fare, and brunch, **Café Beaubourg (68)** (€€) *(100 rue St-Martin, 4th, 01-48.87.63.96; hours: Su–W 8AM–1AM, Th–Sa 8AM–2AM)* faces the esplanade of Beaubourg—and offers its fashionable

patrons a great place from which to people-watch. For classic French dishes that are simple but surprising, **Le Hangar (69)** (€€) *(12 impasse Berthaud, 3rd, 01-42.74.55.44, cash only; hours: Tu–Sa 12PM–3PM, 6:30PM–12AM, closed Aug)*, a cozy bistro by the doll museum, is one of the best values in Paris. Around the corner is another great find: good food and friendly staff are served up at **Le Petit Marcel (70)** (€) *(65 rue Rambuteau, 4th, 01-48.87.10.20; hours: 8AM–1AM)*. **Le 404 (71)** (€€) *(69 rue des Gravilliers, 3rd, 01-42.74.57.81; hours: M–F 12PM–2:30PM, 8PM–2AM, Sa–Su 12PM–4PM brunch, 8PM–2AM)* is a fabulous Moroccan restaurant that's funky, sexy, and noisy; get down with the table-dancing crowd.

Bars & Nightlife:

Andy Wahloo (73) *(69 rue Gravilliers, 3rd, 01-42.71. 20.38; hours: Tu–Su 5PM–2AM)*, a North African bar next door to **Le 404 (71)** *(see page 80)*, has an industrial décor and amicable staff ready to serve beer, cocktails, and hookahs.

WHERE TO SHOP

Contemporary interior decorations at Sentou Galerie (74) *(18 and 24 rue du Pont Louis-Philippe, 4th, 01-42.71.00.01, www.sentou.fr; hours: M 2PM–7PM, Tu–Sa 10AM–7PM)* and its other location Sentou Galerie (75) *(29 rue François-Miron, 4th, 01-42.78.50.60; hours: M 2PM–7PM, Tu–Sa 10AM–7PM)* have become the new classics; you'll find cutting-edge French design here. Nearby is Paris Happy Home (76) *(76 rue François-Miron, 4th, 01-42.77.66.06, www.parishappyhome.com)*, which focuses on leather goods, glassware, ceramics, and furniture by international designers. The store offers design consultations.

Near Beaubourg, at Rag (79) *(83-85 rue St-Martin, 4th, 01-48. 87. 34.64; hours: M–Su 10:30AM–7:30PM; 2nd location: 81 rue St-Honoré, 1st)*, the vintage designer and discount finds are a mixed bag, from casual sweaters to vintage Gucci.

MARAIS

7 to Pont Marie; **1** to St. Paul;
8 to Chemin Vert or St-Sébastien-Froissart

• SNAPSHOT •

Likely the most fascinating quarter of Paris, the Marais is also one of the most beautiful. Its exquisite character comes partially from a successful combination of diverse cultures and styles. Old elegance is embodied in the 17th-century mansions, expertly restored in the 1960s. These coexist harmoniously with boutiques displaying contemporary art, fashion, and culture. At the same time, small artisans and shopkeepers have held their own against the tide of gentrification, as have the old Jewish quarter and other ethnic neighborhoods. The entry of a vibrant gay culture has brought with it renewal and its own fashion and culture. Galleries, original new designers, bookshops, boutiques, and exhibition spaces line streets such as rue Vieille-du-Temple, rue Debelleyme, rue Charlot, rue des Rosiers, and rue du Roi-de-Sicile. The café culture too is strong. The historical landmarks, superb architecture, and romantic narrow streets garnished with coach lamps and ironwork add to the magic of the scene.

PLACES TO SEE
Landmarks:

Just past the **Pont-Marie** and one street in from the river, **Hôtel de Sens (84)** *(1 rue du Figuier, 4th, 01-42.78. 14.60; hours: Tu–F 1:30PM–8:30PM, Sa 10AM–8:30PM)*, now home to the Forney fine arts library, is a rare medieval building built between 1475-1507, its turrets and arches evocative of a time when Bourbons, Guises, and Cardinal de Pellevé occupied the premises. Just westward, at the border of the Jewish quarter, the **Shoah Memorial (85)** *(17 rue Geoffroy-l'Asnier, 4th, 01-42.77. 44.72 www..memorialdelashoah.org; hours: Su–W, F 10AM–6PM, Th 10AM–10PM)*, with its Memorial to the Unknown Jewish Martyr, is a memorial, study center, and museum dedicated to the Holocaust. **Rue des Rosiers**, a once colorful area, is fast being taken over by chain stores, and its old Jewish character is fading. The **Hôtel de Sully (87)** *(62 rue St-Antoine, 4th, 01-42.74.47.75, www. jeudepaume.org; hours: Tu–F 12PM–7PM, Sa–Su 10AM– 7PM)*, a beautiful late-Renaissance mansion, houses the Center for National Monuments.

A step away is the heart of the Marais, the **Place des Vosges (88)** *(rue des Francs Bourgeois, 4th)*. Perhaps the most lovely and aesthetically pleasing square in the world, it's perfectly symmetrical: 36 houses, equally placed on four sides, stand gracefully over rows of arcades. Red brick and stone facades with slate blue roofs and dormer windows lend a simple yet regal elegance to the large square, where jousts, tournaments, and historic events took place. Literati, such as Madame de Sévigné, held salons here. The **Victor Hugo House (89)** *(6 pl. des Vosges, 4th, 01-42.72.10.16; hours: Tu–Su 10AM–6PM)* is where the writer lived and where *Les Misérables* was created. Stroll under the arcades to find a variety of shops, galleries, and cafés—it's where Inspector Maigret of the Simenon detective novels likes to sip a *café-au-lait*.

Explore the many stunning small streets in the area as you make your way northward toward the **Musée Carnavalet (90)** *(23 rue de Sévigné, 3rd, 01-44.59.58.58; hours: Tu–Su 10AM–5:40PM)*, a mansion dedicated to the history of Paris *(see also page 86)*. One street westward, you have the opportunity to enter an old Marais home: the **Musée Cognacq-Jay (91)** *(Hôtel de Donon, 8 rue Elzévir, 4th, 01-40.27.07.21; hours: Tu–Su 10AM–5:40PM)* was once the residence of a prominent businessman and art collector. A short walk away, the

Picasso Museum (92) *(Hôtel Salé, 5 rue de Thorigny, 3rd, 01-42.71.25. 21, www.musee-picasso.fr; hours: Oct–Mar W–M 9:30AM–5:30PM, Apr–Sep W–M 9:30AM–6PM)* is housed in a grand Marais mansion. Picasso admirers are treated to masterpieces in paintings, etchings, and sculptures. Kitty-corner, the **National Archives** are housed in the **Hôtel de Rohan (93)** *(87 rue Vieille-*

du-Temple, 3rd, 01-40.27.60.96; hours: Tu–Su 12PM–6PM) and around the corner in the **Hôtel de Soubise (94)** *(60 rue des Francs-Bourgeois, 3rd, 01-40.27.60.96; hours: M, W–F 10AM–12:30PM, 2PM–5:30PM, Sa–Su 2PM–5:30PM)*; both buildings are marvelous examples of 18th-century architecture. **Cloître des Billettes (54)** *(24 rue des Archives, 4th, 01-40.72.38.79; hours: 11AM–7PM)*, the oldest medieval cloister in Paris, was built in 1427 for the Brothers of Charity. The courtyard, with its Gothic galleries, colonnaded arches, and arcades topped by graceful vaults, is especially appealing. The cloister presents work by emerging artists; exhibits change twice a month and are usually free. Be sure to stroll along the **rue Vieille-du-Temple (95)** *(rue de Rivoli/rue de Poitou, 3rd/4th)*—its charm comes not only from the 13th-century medieval houses but also from the street's many luxury shops. Further to the west, around **rue Ste-Croix-de-la-Bretonnerie (96)** *(rue de Temple/rue Vieille de Temple, 4th)*, is the **gay district** ("pink triangle"), a vibrant, stylish scene replete with hotels, bars, clubs, and restaurants.

Arts & Entertainment:

Magicians ply their trade outside the wonderful **Museum of Magic (97)** *(11 rue St-Paul, 4th, 01-42.72.13.26, www.museedelamagie.com; hours: W, Sa–Su 2PM–7PM)*; inside, they demonstrate with museum pieces. In a magnificent mansion, the **Maison Européenne de la Photographie (98)** *(5-7 rue de Fourcy, 4th, 01-44.78.75.00, www.mep-fr.org; hours: W–Su 11AM–8PM)* houses more than 15,000 works of contemporary photography;

and its café is super-chic. The 140-room **Musée Carnavalet (90)** *(see also page 84)* covers the history of Paris, through paintings, sculptures, documents, objects, and memorabilia. Some samplings of what is on view are: a piece of the Bastille prison, lithographs, porcelain vases, and Proust's reconstructed cork-lined bedroom (where he wrote most of *A la recherche du temps perdu*, *Remembrance of Things Past*). On a more human scale, the refined **Musée Cognacq-Jay (91)** *(see also page 84)* is home to a once private collection of 18th-century art and furniture. The **Picasso Museum (92)** *(see also page 84)* has an astonishing collection of work from all periods of the artist's long and diverse career. **La Galerie d'Architecture (99)** *(11 rue des Blancs-Manteaux, 4th, 01-49.96.64.00, www.galerie-architecture.fr; hours: Tu–Sa 11AM–7PM)* shows the work of contemporary architects against a clean, crisp, white backdrop.

PLACES TO EAT & DRINK
Where to Eat:

La Victoire Suprème du Coeur (15) (€) *(27-31 rue du Bourg-Tibourg, 4th, 01-40.41.95.03, www.vscoeur.com; hours: M–F 12PM–3PM, 6:30PM–10:30PM, Sa 12PM–11PM, Su 12PM–10:30PM)* is a vegetarian restaurant that caters to those with "health" on the mind. Supposedly the first wine bar in Paris, **Le Coude Fou (65)** (€–€€) *(12 rue du Bourg-Tibourg, 4th, 01-42.77.15.16, www.lecoudefou.com; hours: 12PM–2AM)* is friendly and intimate with food better than the usual wine bar fare. The best afternoon tea outside London is to be had at

Mariage Frères (66) (€-€€) *(30 rue du Bourg-Tibourg, 4th, 01-42.72.28.11, www.mariagefreres.com; hours: 12PM–7PM, tea counters & museums 10:30AM–7:30PM).* A gem of haute cuisine, **L'Ambroisie (100)** (€€€€) *(9 pl. des Vosges, 4th, 01-42.78.51.45; hours: Tu–Sa 12PM–1:45PM, 8PM–9:45PM, closed Feb & end July–end Aug)* is said to be one of the most beautiful restaurants in Paris. The food is spectacular while the décor is ornate and Versailles-like; the unique experience is worth the steep price. For a less refined evening, **L'Auberge de Jarente (101)** (€-€€) *(7 rue Jarente, 4th, 01-42.77.49.35; hours: Tu–Sa 12PM–2:30PM, 7:30PM–10:30PM)* is casual, friendly, and serves hearty Basque food. At **Au Bourguignon du Marais (102)** (€€) *(52 rue François-Miron, 4th, 01-48.87.15.40; hours: M–Sa 12PM–11PM)* the excellent selection of Burgundy goes with its classic bistro fare. Best for cakes and tea, **Le Loir dans la Théière (105)** (€) *(3 rue des Rosiers, 4th, 01-42.72.90.61; hours: M–F 11:30AM–7PM, Sa–Su 10AM–7PM)* is funky and cool; inspired by *Alice in Wonderland*, its name means "The Dormous in the Teapot." While the Jewish character of **rue des Rosiers** may be on the wane, the African soul of nearby **rue Elzévir** is flourishing.

Senegalese and African dishes and delicacies are on the menu at **Le Petit Dakar (106)** (€) *(6 rue Elzévir, 3rd, 01-44.59.34.74, www.csao.fr; hours: M–Sa12PM–2:30PM, 7:30PM–10:30PM, closed Aug)*; try the silky palm hearts and sweet-and-sour chicken and lemon stew. For arguably the best couscous in Paris, try **Chez Omar (108)** (€€) *(47 rue de Bretagne, 3rd, 01-42.72.36.26; hours: M–Sa 12PM–2:30PM, 7PM– 11:30PM, Su 7PM–11:30PM)*, a North African favorite among the cognoscenti. The combination Maghreb-French cuisine is worth the wait in line.

Bars & Nightlife:

You might expect Edith Piaf to saunter into **Le Connétable (72)** *(55 rue des Archives, 3rd, 01-42.77.41.40; hours: M–Sa 11AM–3PM, 7PM–3AM)*: it's a typical Parisian bar, chatty regulars and all. Vibrant sounds in music—from cabaret to jazz to fusion—emanate from **Les 7 Lézards (109)** *(10 rue des Rosiers, 4th, 01-48.87.08.97, www.7 lezards.com; hours: opens 6PM, jazz sets begin 9PM)*. **Le Jokko (110)** *(5 rue Elzévir, 3rd, 01-42.74.35.96, www.csao.fr; call for hours)* is an African-themed bar and exhibition space featuring live music. At the literary wine bar **La Belle Hortense (111)** *(31 rue Vieille-du-Temple, 4th, 01-48.04.71.60, www.cafeine.com; hours: 5PM–2AM)*, sip a glass of red wine and peruse a book from the window ledges. For some, wine's a game; at **L'Apparement Café (112)** *(18 rue des Coutures-St-Gervais, 3rd, 01-48.87.12.22; hours: 12PM–2AM)* wine goes with the game: you can play cards or a board game while sipping your *verre de rouge*. Further south in the **gay district**, (also known as the "pink triangle"), **L'Open Café (113)** *(17 rue des Archives, 4th, 01-42.72.26.18, www.opencafe.fr; hours: Su–Th*

11AM–2AM, F–Sa 11AM–4AM) is a favorite gay café and a happening night spot. Mixed gay-straight techno-lovers crowd the floor of **Le Mixer (114)** *(23 rue Ste-Croix-de-la-Bretonnerie, 4th, 01-48.87.55.44, www.mixerbar.com; hours: 5PM–12AM)*. Straight-friendly gay locale **Amnésia Café (115)** *(42 rue Vieille-du-Temple, 4th, 01-42.72.16.94; hours: Su–Th 11AM–2AM, F–Sa 11AM–3AM)* gets rowdy at night; they serve drinks, sandwiches, and brunch. Nearby, long-standing **Le Central (116)** *(33 rue Vieille-du-Temple, 4th, 01-48.87.99.33, hotelcentral marais.monsite.wanadoo.fr; hours: M–F 4PM–2AM, Sa–Su 2PM–2AM)* is a cozy spot for natives and travelers alike.

WHERE TO SHOP

Julian Schnabel's art adorns the walls of the showroom loft of Tunisian-born Azzedine Alaïa (77) *(7 rue de Moussy, 4th, 01-42.72.19.19)*, emphasizing that the sexy, form-fitting clothes are wearable art. Colorful tweeds and woolens, Audrey Hepburn-style, make Blancs Manteaux (78) *(42 rue des Blancs Manteaux, 4th, 01-42.71.00.00, www.blancsmanteaux.com)* a find; its wares are mostly shipped, so the shop is more of a depot. Stroll through the 60 or so shops of antiques and bric-a-brac dealers at Village St-Paul (117) *(along rue St-Paul, near rue Charlemagne, 4th; hours: Th–M 11AM–7PM)*. Senteurs de Fée (120) *(10 rue de Sévigné, 3rd, 01-44.54. 97.27)* stocks incense.

Rue des Francs-Bourgeois is a great shopping street. Fabulous white linen and stretchy laces are elegant and comfortable at Anne Fontaine (122) *(12 rue des Francs-Bourgeois, 3rd, 01-44.59.81.59, www.annefontaine.com)*. Enter Ali Baba's cave, full of fabulous Tunisian homeware, at 2 Mille et 1 Nuits (123) *(13 rue des Francs-Bourgeois, 4th, 01-48.87.07.07, www.2001nuits.com)*. Zadig & Voltaire (125) *(42 rue des Francs-Bourgeois, 3rd, 01-44.54.00.60, www.zadig-et-voltaire.com)*, with branches around the city, is popular for its casual, urban wardrobe offerings. Issey Miyake's innovative textile design is evident at A-poc (126) *(47 rue des Francs-Bourgeois, 4th, 01-44.54.07.05, www.isseymiyake.com)*; the name is derived from "a piece of cloth," the concept being to design wearable art from one piece of fabric.

Painted chests and armoires abound among the refurbished 18th- and 19th-century furniture at Meubles Peints (127) *(32 rue Sévigné, 4th, 01-42.77.54.60, www.meublespeints.com)*. Photo buffs will flock to fashion photography bookshop Comptoir de l'Image (128) *(44 rue de Sévigné, 3rd, 01-42.72.03.92)* and Galerie Chez Valentin (129) *(9 rue St-Gilles, 3rd, 01-48.87.42.55)*, which exhibits experimental video, photography, and installations. African art and crafts are on display at La Boutique de la CSAO (130) *(9 rue Elzévir, 3rd, 01-42.71.33.17, www.csao.fr; hours: M–Sa 11AM–1PM, 2PM–7PM)*, and contemporary African art at La Galerie 3A (131) *(9 rue Elzévir,*

3rd, 01-42.77.66.42, www.csao.fr; hours: M–Sa 11AM–1PM, 2–7PM). Wispy fabrics, inventive details, and incredible use of color have given the Japanese fashion designer **Tsumori Chisato (132)** *(20 rue Barbette, 3rd, 01-42.78.18.88)* a dedicated fan base in Paris. The **Bains du Marais (133)** *(31-33 rue des Blancs-Manteaux, 4th, 01-44.61.02.02, www. lesbainsdumarais.com)* offers a break from the wear and tear of sightseeing and shopping. Open to women Monday through Wednesday *(M 11AM–8PM, Tu 11AM–11PM, W 10AM–7PM)*; open to men Thursday and Friday *(Th 11AM–11PM, F 10AM–8PM)*; and open to both on Wednesday evenings and weekends *(W 7PM–11PM, Sa 10AM–8PM, Su 11AM–11PM)*, the spa gives divine hamman treatments. Or you can combine a facial with manicure, pedicure, haircut, or another salon offering.

Rue Vieille-du-Temple (95) is another treasure trove for shopping. Limited-edition designer tableware gives new meaning to glassware and crockery at **Chône (135)** *(60 rue Vieille-du-Temple, 3rd, 01-44.78.90.00)*. Chocolates and pastries reign at **Cacao et Chocolat (136)** *(36 rue Vieille-du-Temple, 4th, 01-42.71.50.06)*.

For carefully crafted books on international architecture, art, and design, try **Archibooks (138)** *(18-20 rue de la Perle, 3rd, 01-42.25.15.58, www.archibooks.com)*. A few streets up from the **Picasso Museum (92)** *(see also page 84),* find fine ceramics and porcelain at Galerie Pierre (139) *(22 rue Debelleyme, 3rd, 01-42.72.20.24)*. Hunt for great discounts at L'Habilleur (140) *(44 rue de Poitou, 3rd, 01-48.87.77.12)*: end-of-line designer pieces and hot-off-the-runway creations are 50%-70% off. Rue Charlot (141) *(beginning at rue des Quatre Fils, 3rd)* has been inventively redone, harboring galleries, bookshops, cafés, and shops, such as **Passage de Retz** *(No. 9)*, **Food** *(No. 58)*, and **Moon Young Hee** *(No. 62)*.

WHERE TO STAY

Hôtel Bourg Tibourg (81) *(€€-€€€) (19 rue du Bourg-Tibourg, 4th, 01-42.78.47.39, www.hotelbourg tibourg.com)*—part of the Costes Brothers' empire—is dramatic, sensual, and intimate; silk and taffeta, fringes and tassels, the hotel is a tasteful combination of styles, textures, and colors reminiscent of the private inner chambers of a princely retreat. A revamped 17th-century town house, Hôtel de la Bretonnerie (82) *(€-€€) (22 rue Ste-Croix-de-la-Bretonnerie, 4th, 01-48.87.77.63, www.bretonnerie.com)* is comfortable, tasteful, and a good value. In the budget category, Hôtel de Nice (83) *(€) (42 bis, rue de Rivoli, 4th, 01-42.78.55.29, www.hotel denice.com)* is filled with "busy" patterns and textiles and has its space challenges, but is a good bargain and is well located.

Near the Jewish quarter at the Hôtel Caron de Beaumarchais (142) *(€-€€) (12 rue Vieille-du-Temple,*

4th, 01-42.72.34.12, www.carondebeaumarchais.com)
the service is impeccable; small rooms with 18th-century
décor are prepared with great attention to detail. A good
find at a reasonable price (especially for the neighborhood), Grand Hôtel Malher (143) (€-€€) *(5 rue Malher,
4th, 01-42.72.60.92, www.grandhotelmalher.com)* is
comfortable and well run. Simple and unassuming,
Hôtel Jeanne d'Arc (144) (€) *(3 rue Jarente, 4th, 01-
48.87.62.11, www.parishotels.com)* is a great budget
hotel. Modern and medieval, the luxury hotel Pavillon
de la Reine (145) (€€€-€€€€) *(28 pl. des Vosges, 3rd, 01-
40.29.19.19, www.pavillon-de-la-reine.com)* has breathtaking views. Small is beautiful at Hôtel de la Place des
Vosges (146) (€-€€) *(12 rue de Birague, 4th, 01-
42.72.60.46, www.hotelplacedesvosges.com),* and accommodations are well maintained; the remodeled rooms
have hardwood floors, wooden beams, and exposed
stone walls (ask for the "discovery rate" for roughly a
25% discount on the new rooms). Close by, Hôtel
Turenne Le Marais (147) (€-€€) *(6 rue de Turenne, 4th,
01-42.78.43.25, www.turennemarais.com)* is part of a
hotel chain; rooms are color coordinated and charming.
Nearer the Musée Carnavalet (90) and Picasso Museum
(92), Hôtel des Chevaliers (148) (€-€€) *(30 rue de Turenne,
3rd, 01-42.72.73.47, www.chevaliers-paris-hotel.com)*
has small but comfortable rooms. If you love Christian
Lacroix clothes, you'll love the profusion of color in his
room designs at Hôtel du Petit Moulin (149) (€€-€€€)
*(29/31 rue de Poitou, 3rd, 01-42.74.10.10, www.
hotelpetitmoulinparis.com).*

MAP CONTINUES AT LEFT

la
République

ubaud
OBERKAMPF
(5,9)
russol

kampf (42)

MÉNILMONTANT (2)

av. Parmentier

r. St-Maur

Oberkampf

PARMENTIER (3)

r. Crespin du Gast

av. Jean Aicard

r. des Bluets

bd. de Ménilmontant

des Panoyaux

r. des Tlemcen

r. Houdan

av. des Nanettes

ST-MAUR (3)

39

r. de la Folie Méricourt

psg. Beslay

r. Pasteur

ST-MAUR (3)

av. de la République

PÈRE LACHAISE (2,3)

ÉBASTIEN SSART
r. St-Sébastien

r. St-Ambroise

ST-AMBROISE (9)

r. Ladharrière

sq. Maurice Gardette

du Chemin Vert

r. Merlin

Duranti

N

RICHARD LENOIR (5)

A. Baudin

r. Pelée

r. de l'Asile Popincourt

r. Mouffe

av. Parmentier

r. Pétion

r. St-Maur

r. Servan

sq. de la Roquette

7

psg. Ste-Anne Popincourt

Chemin Vert

r. Popincourt

bd. Voltaire

C. Desmoulins

r. de la Roquette

de la Croix Faubin

r. Gerbier

r. de la Folie Regnault

VERT
r. du Richard Lenoir

r. Fronmon

r. Bréguet

r. Sedaine

VOLTAIRE (9)

r. Auguste Laurent

r. Mercoeur

r. Léon Frot

r. de Belfort

BRÉGUET SABIN (5)

bd. Richard Lenoir

22

BASTILLE

psg. Charles Dallery

r. Basfroi

r. Godefroy Cavaignac

Richard Lenoir

CHARONNE (9)

bd. Voltaire

28

21 29

r. de la Roquette

psg. Thiéré

27

r. des Taillandiers

Keller

23

Ledru Rollin

Dallery

r. Jules Vallès

20

18

r. de Lappe

r. de

15

Charonne

r. Jean Macé

Chanzy

RUE DES BOULETS (9)

1

24

2

19

13

2

34 30

3

r. du Faubourg

LEDRU ROLLIN (8)

St-Antoine

r. de la Forge Royale

r. St-Bernard

r. Trousseau

12

11

r. Paul Bert

14

r. de Montreuil

Tillon

31

r. Biscornet

r. de Lyon

r. Lacuée

r. J. César

r. Moreau

St-Nicolas

r. de Prague

Ch. Baudelaire

Rousse

r. d'Aligre

4

r. Crozatier

r. de Citeaux

Beccaria

FAIDHERBE CHALIGNY (8)

Chaligny

r. de Reuilly

10

Claude Tillier

Ledru Rollin

av. Daumesnil

25

r. M. Chasles

7

r. Parrot

r. Hector Malot

REUILLY DIDEROT (1,8)

Rondelet

bd. Diderot

GARE DE LYON (1,14)

r. Traversière

bd. Diderot

Berey

6

GARE DE LYON (A,D)

0   0.25 mile

0   0.25 km

chapter 4

BASTILLE

CANAL ST-MARTIN

BASTILLE
CANAL ST-MARTIN

Places to See:

1. Place de la Bastille
2. Colonne de Juillet
3. Opéra Bastille
4. Marché d'Aligre
5. Pavillon de l'Arsenal
32. Rue du Faubourg-du-Temple
33. St-Louis Hospital
34. Port de l'Arsenal

Places to Eat & Drink:

6. Le Train Bleu
7. Le Viaduc Café
8. Le Square Trousseau
10. Chez Ramulaud
11. Le Temps au Temps
12. L'Ecailler du Bistrot
13. Le Bistrot Paul Bert
14. Au Vieux Chêne
15. Pause Café
16. Le Souk
17. Le C'Amelot
18. Le Balajo
19. Le Café du Passage
20. La Muse Vin
21. Le Wax
22. Café de l'Industrie
35. Chez Prune

36. La Marine
37. Favela Chic
38. Hôtel du Nord
39. Le Villaret
40. Le Verre Volé
41. L'Atmosphère
42. Le Vin de Zinc

Where to Shop:

9. Serge Amoruso
23. Viaduc des Arts
24. Isabel Marant
25. Gaëlle Barré
26. Anne Willi
27. Come On Eileen
43. Artazart
44. Stella Cadente
45. Antoine et Lili

Where to Stay:

28. Hôtel Lyon-Mulhouse
29. Daval Hôtel
30. Hôtel le Pavillon Bastille
31. Maison Zen
46. Hôtel Notre-Dame
47. Hôtel Plessis
48. Hôtel de Nevers

BASTILLE

1 5 8 *to Bastille;* **8** *to Ledru-Rollin;*
1 14 *to Gare de Lyon;* **5 9** *to Oberkampf*

• SNAPSHOT •

The Bastille prison stormed by the people on July 14,
1789, during the French Revolution, no longer exists,
though pieces of it can be seen in the Musée Carnavalet
(see Chapter 3, page 84). However, its ghosts seem to
hover over the quarter, reminding us of the power of the
people. The Place de la Bastille became a marker dividing
central Paris from the working-class neighborhoods in
the eastern part of the city. Recently gentrified, the
Bastille district has become a center of activity, from the
Opéra Bastille to the burgeoning cafés and shops. Bistros
and restaurants abound; many retain their working-class
flavor with a twist while others bring in a new air.

PLACES TO SEE
Landmarks:

The French Revolution was followed decades later by
other revolts. To commemorate those killed during the
uprisings of 1830 and 1848, a bronze column was

erected in the center of the
Place de la Bastille (1) *(bd.
Beaumarchais/rue du Faubourg,
4th)*: the **Colonne de Juillet (2)**
(pl. de la Bastille, 4th) bears the
names of many buried in the

crypt beneath the column. At its apex is the statue "The Genius of Liberty." The **Opéra Bastille (3)** *(130 rue de Lyon, 12th, 01-72.29.35.35, www.operadeparis.fr; box office hours: M–Sa 10:30AM–6:30PM)*, officially opened by President Mitterand on Bastille Day 1989 as part of the celebrations of the Bicentennial of the French Revolution, is as far removed from the Opéra Garnier as imaginable yet still retains a majesty of its own. The façade is glass while the interior is granite with an amazing glass ceiling. A feat of technological innovation, it houses five movable stages. At the opposite end of the spectrum, the nearby **Marché d'Aligre (4)** *(pl. d'Aligre, 12th, marchedaligre.free.fr; hours: stalls, Tu–Su 8AM–1PM; covered market & shops, Tu–Sa 8AM–1PM, 4PM–7:30PM, Su 8AM–1PM)*, a frolicking food market with secondhand antique stalls, embodies the working-class character of the area.

Arts & Entertainment:

In addition to its opera season, **Opéra Bastille (3)** *(see also above)* offers free lunchtime events ("Casse-Croûte à l'Opéra") every Thursday. The **Pavillon de l'Arsenal (5)** *(21 bd. Morland, 4th, 01-42.76.33.97, www.pavillon-arsenal.com; hours: Tu–Sa 10:30AM–6:30PM, Su 11AM–7PM)*, in an old 19th-century iron and glass warehouse, covers the urban development and architectural history of Paris through photos, descriptions, and scale models; in individual video booths you can watch any of 120 films about

Paris's architects and their work, or watch a film about the city in the video lounge. You can also catch one of the temporary exhibits of big names in architecture. Check out exhibits of contemporary artists at galleries in **rue de Charonne**, **rue de Lappe**, and **rue Keller**.

PLACES TO EAT & DRINK
Where to Eat:

At **Le Train Bleu (6)** **(€€-€€€)** *(pl. Louis Armand, 12th, inside Gare de Lyon train station, 1st Floor, opp. F platforms, 01-44.75.76.76, www.le-train-bleu.com; hours: 11:30AM–3PM, 7PM–11PM, book ahead)* ambience is everything: the murals and frescoed ceilings of this fabulous Belle-Époque brasserie will transport you. It's OK to have just a glass of champagne and stare at the walls. The Bastille area is surrounded by good, affordable bistros, once the staple of working-class life and now destinations for trendy aficionados and locals alike. **Le**

Viaduc Café (7) **(€€)** *(43 ave. Daumesnil, 12th, 01-44.74.70.70, www.viaduc-café.fr; hours: 8AM–2AM, food served 12PM–3PM, 7PM–11PM)*, under the renovated railroad viaduct, is pretty and noisy, with lots of pavement tables; best for its Sunday jazz brunch. Put together fabulous Belle-Époque décor, creative cuisine, and a rising neighborhood chic factor, and you get supermodels and other celebs swarming to **Le Square Trousseau (8)** **(€€)** *(1 rue Antoine Vollon, 12th, 01-43.43.06.00; hours: Tu–Sa*

12PM–2:30PM, 8PM–11:30PM). The stylishness of **Chez Ramulaud (10)** (€€) *(269 rue Faubourg-St-Antoine, 11th, 01-43.72.23.29; call for hours, closed Sa lunch & Su dinner)* has contributed to its growing popularity; pols and activists are among the clientele. Three restaurants stand out in **rue Paul-Bert** for consistently good food, excellent wine, and great atmosphere: **Le Temps au Temps (11)** (€-€€) *(13 rue Paul-Bert, 11th, 01-43. 79.63.40, www.tempsautemps.com; hours: T–Sa, 12PM– 2PM, 8PM–10:30PM, closed Aug)*, small and cozy with good contemporary cuisine; **L'Ecailler du Bistrot (12)** (€- €€) *(22 rue Paul-Bert, 11th, 01-43.72.76.77; hours: Tu–Sa to 11PM, closed Aug)*, maybe the best fish and seafood bistro in Paris, famous for its oysters; and **Le Bistrot Paul Bert (13)** (€€) *(18 rue Paul-Bert, 11th, 01- 43.72.24.01; hours: Tu–Th 12PM–2PM, 7:30PM–11PM, F–Sa 12PM–2PM, 7:30PM–11:30PM)*, old-fashioned and simple, with generous portions and an owner who'll talk about wine at the drop of a hat. Recalling the 1930s, **Au Vieux Chêne (14)** (€€) *(7 rue Dahomey, 11th, 01-43.71.67.69; hours: M–F 12PM–2PM, 8PM–10:30PM, Sa 8PM– 10:30PM)* is a handsome bistro that's just the right fit for your antique-crawling expedition. **Pause Café (15)** (€- €€) *(41 rue de Charonne, 11th, 01-48. 06.80.33; hours: M–Sa 7:30AM–2AM, Su 9AM–8PM)* is welcoming with lots of outdoor seating; try the tomato and cucumber soup, and chicken sautéed in coconut milk and basil. Those trendsetters and rockers love the couscous at

Le Souk (16) (€-€€) *(1 rue Keller, 11th, 01-49.29.05.08; hours: Tu–F 7:30PM–11:30PM, Sa 12PM–2:30PM, 7:30PM–12AM, Su 12PM–2:30PM, 7:30PM–11:30PM);* you might admire the covered bazaar ambience of this Moroccan restaurant. Though there's no choice on the menu, **Le C'Amelot (17) (€€)** *(50 rue Amelot, 11th, 01-43.55.54.04; hours: 12PM–2PM, 7:30PM–11PM)* serves sophisticated bistro cuisine at budget prices. **Le Villaret (39) (€€)** *(13 rue Ternaux, 11th, 01-43.57.89.76; hours: M–Sa to 12AM, closed Sa lunch & Aug)* is a fabulous neighborhood bistro with creative renditions of classic French cuisine; the crowds you're likely to find there will have a mix of wine connoisseurs, neighborhood old hats, and a sprinkling of hipsters.

Bars & Nightlife:

The oldest *musette* dance hall in Paris, **Le Balajo (18)** *(9 rue de Lappe, 11th, 01-47.00.07.87, www.balajo.fr; times vary, call for hours)* has an old-fashioned atmosphere that appeals, with 1950s, 1960s, 1970s music, salsa, and disco on varying nights. Come before the gig, and you

can take a dancing class. **Rue de Charonne** is full of cafés and wine bars. The relaxed, romantic **Le Café du Passage (19)** *(12 rue de Charonne, 11th, 01-49. 29.97.64; hours: Su–F 6PM–2AM, Sa 12PM–2AM)* offers more than 300 wines of great vintages. **La Muse Vin (20)** *(101 rue de Charonne, 11th, 01-40.09.93.05, www.lamuse vin.com; hours: M–Sa 11AM–11PM)* is a "natural" wine bar (organic wine made without industrial additives), with wines mostly unknown in the U.S. (beware the heavy cigarette smoke). At the bar **Le Wax (21)** *(15 rue Daval, 11th, 01-40.21.16.16; hours: Tu–Th to 2AM, F–Sa to 5AM)* the décor is a throwback to the psychedelic 1960s. Of the plentiful cool cafés around the Bastille, **Café de l'Industrie (22)** *(16 rue St-Sabin, 11th, 01-47.00.13.53, www.cafedelindustrie.com; hours: 9:30AM–2AM)*, a local haunt, is one of the cheeriest and friendliest. The wine bar **Le Vin de Zinc (42)** *(25 rue Oberkampf, 11th, 01-48.06.28.23; call for hours)* offers all the favorite reds and whites, mostly without sulphates (to prevent those pesky headaches); they also serve large portions of hearty foods, like steak and fries.

WHERE TO SHOP

Renovated and glassed in, the arcades of an old railway viaduct house the Viaduc des Arts (23) *(1-129 ave. Daumesnil, 12th, www.viaduc-des-arts.com)*, with its craft shops, galleries, exhibition spaces, and open *ateliers* where artisans weave and hammer, stitch and iron. Notable among them: **Créations Chérif** *(No. 13)*, with sofas and chairs; **VIA** *(Valorisation de l'Innovation dans l'Ameublement, Nos. 29-37)*, exhibiting textiles, furniture, and home accessories; **Home Intra** *(No. 47)*, with home furnishings, drapes, tapestries, and upholstering to order or ready-made; **Série Rare** *(No. 121)* for fabulous bronze doorknobs, tie-backs, and other architectural fittings inspired by antiquity; and **Jean-Charles Brosseau** *(No. 129)*, designer *extraordinaire* of perfumes and hats. There are real "finds" among the secondhand merchandise at the **Marché d'Aligre (4)** *(see also page 97)*. Isabel Marant (24) *(16 rue de Charonne, 11th, 01-49.29.71.55)* designs feminine clothing in silks, cashmere, and other fine fabrics. In **rue Keller**, the seductive mohair creations of Gaëlle Barré (25) *(17 rue Keller, 11th, 01-43.14.63.02)* will turn your head. A few doors away, Anne Willi (26) *(13 rue Keller, 11th, 01-48.06.74.06)* designs are elegant and versatile. With three floors of vintage delight at Come On Eileen (27) *(16-18 rue des Taillandiers, 11th, 01-43.38.12.11; hours: M–F 11AM–8:30PM, Su 2PM–8PM)*, pieces range from funky cowboy duds to Hermès scarves. The handmade leather goods at Serge Amoruso (9) *(13 rue Abel, 12th, 01-43.45.14.10, www.sergeamoruso. com)* are a labor of love; watch the artisans as they perform magic in the workshop.

WHERE TO STAY

Hotels are less expensive in this working-class area. Rooms are plain, spare, but sizable at Hôtel Lyon-Mulhouse (28) (€) *(8 bd. Beaumarchais, 11th, 01-47.00.91. 50, www.1-hotel-paris.com)* and some have lovely views. Functional rooms with A/C and access to the galleries, cafés, and boutiques of the area make Daval Hôtel (29) (€) *(21 rue Daval, 11th, 01-47.00.51.23, www.hoteldaval.com)* a good budget choice. A hop away from the Opéra Bastille, Hôtel le Pavillon Bastille (30) (€€) *(65 rue de Lyon, 12th, 01-43.43.65.65, www.hotels-paris-pavillonbastille.com)*, with its blue and yellow color scheme and young, friendly staff, is bright and cheery; no A/C makes traffic noise on street-side rooms problematic. An alternative is a studio apart-ment at the Maison Zen (31) (€) *(35 rue de Lyon, 12th, 01-77.11.13. 36, www.maisonzen.com, cheap weekly rates, credit cards not accept-ed)* sunny, whitewashed units with Ikea furnishings surround a tree-lined cobblestone courtyard. Close to the Place de la République, Hôtel Notre-Dame (46) (€) *(51 rue de Malte, 11th, 01-47.00.78.76, www.hotel-notre dame.com)* offers minimal comfort but is clean; some rooms have no bathrooms. Hôtel Plessis (47) (€) *(25 rue du Grand Prieuré, 11th, 01-47.00.13.38, www.paris-hotel-plessis.com)* also provides clean, adequate rooms, though a few share bathrooms. A very cheap sleep will rescue the budget weary at Hôtel de Nevers (48) (€) *(53 rue de Malte, 11th, 01-47.00.56.18, www.hoteldenevers. com)*; it's clean but furnishings consist basically of a bed only, and bathrooms are shared.

CANAL ST-MARTIN

③ ⑤ ⑧ ⑨ ⑪ *to République;*
⑤ *to Jacques Bonsergent;* ② *to Colonel Fabien;*
⑦ *to Château Landon or Louis Blanc;*
② ⑤ ⑦ᵇⁱˢ *to Jaurès;* ② ⑤ ⑦ *to Stalingrad*

• SNAPSHOT •

With Marais rents soaring, emerging designers, artists, and media start-ups are moving northward to the increasingly hip and bohemian Canal St-Martin. Overwhelmingly for the young (20- and 30-some-things), the area is fast becoming the "in" place. Its less frenetic pace gives it a village atmosphere with urban sophistication. The three-mile canal, a Seine shortcut, is fascinating to observe as boats maneuver adroitly through locks and under bridges.

PLACES TO SEE
Landmarks:

From the **Place de la República** all the way up to the end of the canal at **Bassin de la Villette**, the work-ing-class underpinnings of the Canal St-Martin area are evident. The houses, taverns, cafés, ware-houses, and factories all reveal

aspects of that 19th-century world. In the **rue du Faubourg-du-Temple (32)** *(starting at pl. de la République,*

19th-century world. In the **rue du Faubourg-du-Temple (32)** *(starting at pl. de la République, 10th)*, a busy street full of ethnic shops and restaurants, details on some buildings and storefronts testify to the care taken in embellishing this working-class neighborhood. However, even the 17th-century **St-Louis Hospital (33)** *(1 ave. Claude-Vellefaux, 10th, 01-42.49.49.49, www.chu-stlouis.fr)*, beautiful though it is, has none of the luxurious ornamentation of the more aristocratic Right Bank districts bordering the river. The best way to see the area is to take a **boat trip** up the canal, passing under romantic footbridges and through its nine locks: you board a Canauxrama boat at **Port de l'Arsenal (34)** *(opposite 50 bd. de la Bastille, 12th, 01-42.39.15.00 for a 3-hour ride; see Bastille neighborhood on the map; at northern end of canal, board at Bassin de la Villette, 13 quai de la Loire, 19th)*. Alternatively, walking along the **Quai de Valmy** or **Quai de Jemmapes** is a relaxed way of absorbing young, cutting-edge Paris and the making of chic.

PLACES TO EAT & DRINK
Where to Eat:

With the Canal St-Martin attracting converts, "funk" is in and **Chez Prune (35) (€)** *(71 quai de Valmy/36 rue Beaurepaire, 10th, 01-42.41.30.47; hours: M–Sa 8AM–2AM, Su 10AM–2AM, hot food 12PM–3PM, snacks 7PM–11PM, Su brunch 12PM–4PM)* has become a prime example of a trendy café-bar. Eclectic and unpretentious, its strongest appeal is the view over the canal on the **Quai de Valmy**. Another café popular in this youthful neighborhood is **La Marine (36) (€-€€)** *(55 bis, quai de Valmy,*

10th, 01-42.39.69.81 or 01-42.39.03.78; hours: open to 12AM). Brazilian home-style food at **Favela Chic (37)** (€€)

(18 rue du Faubourg-du-Temple, 11th, 01-40.21.38.14, www.favela chic.com; hours: Tu–Th to 2AM, F–Sa to 4AM) mixed with irresistible music will have you dancing between courses. Romantic **Hôtel du Nord (38)** (€-€€) *(102 quai de Jemmapes, 10th, 01-40.40.78.78; hours: open to 12AM),* where the 1938 film of the same name was shot, is an idyllic spot overlooking a footbridge of the canal. In the evenings it swings with live music.

Bars & Nightlife:

Tiny and simple, **Le Verre Volé (40)** *(67 rue de Lancry, 10th, 01-48.03.17.34, www.leverrevole.fr; call for hours)* is a combination wine bar, bistro, and wine shop. Off **Quai de Valmy**, the eclectic bar **L'Atmosphère (41)** *(49 rue Lucien-Sampaix, 10th, 01-40.38.09.21; hours: 10AM–2AM)* has seating outdoors along the canal, which allows you to soak up the atmosphere, and live music Sunday afternoons. **Hôtel du Nord (38)** *(see top of this page; entertainment reservations, 01-53.19.98.88)* features live jazz Wednesday nights, cabaret songs Fridays, and a singer Saturdays. Twice a month, comedy is performed in English.

WHERE TO SHOP

Walk along the canal or browse the shops on **Quai de Valmy**. Books and magazines on art, architecture, and design abound at Artazart (43) (*83 quai de Valmy, 10th, 01-40.40.24.00/03, www.artazart.com; hours: M–F 10:30AM–7:30PM, Sa–Su 2 PM–8PM*), which also hosts photo exhibits. The young designer behind Stella Cadente (44) (*93 quai de Valmy, 10th, 01-42.09.27.00, www.stella-cadente.com; hours: 11AM–7:30PM*) has a flair for the romantic, with chiffon, feathers, and beads galore. Bright is the key word at Antoine et Lili (45) (*95 quai de Valmy, 10th, 01-40.37.34.86, www.antoine etlili.com, clothes 01-40.37.41.55, home design 01-40.37.34.86, children's 01-40.37.58.14*). Its shops around Paris and abroad feature home design, fashion, and accessories; there's a café too, when you need to get off your feet.

chapter 5

LATIN QUARTER
ÎLE DE LA CITÉ
ÎLE ST-LOUIS

LATIN QUARTER
ÎLE DE LA CITÉ
ÎLE ST-LOUIS

Places to See:

1. Place St-Michel
2. Shakespeare & Co.
3. St-Julien-le-Pauvre
4. St-Séverin
5. National Museum of the Middle Ages (Cluny Museum)
6. Sorbonne
7. Collège de France
8. Panthéon
9. Place de la Contrescarpe
10. Rue Mouffetard
11. Paris Mosque
12. Jardin des Plantes
13. National Museum of Natural History
14. Arènes de Lutèce
15. Institute of the Arab World
57. Square du Vert-Galant
58. Place Dauphine
59. Palais de Justice
60. SAINTE-CHAPELLE ★
61. Conciergerie
62. Flower and Bird Market
63. Crypte Archéologique
64. NOTRE-DAME ★
65. Museum of Notre-Dame de Paris
67. Hôtel Chernizot
68. Hôtel Lambert
69. St-Louis-en-l'Ile

Places to Eat & Drink:

16. La Fourmi Ailée
17. Le Reminet
18. L'Atelier Maître Albert
19. Le Pré Verre
20. Brasserie Balzar
21. Chantairelle
22. Le Berthoud
23. Les Fontaines
24. Le Perraudin
25. Café de la Nouvelle Mairie
26. Les Cinq Saveurs d'Anada
27. L'Assiette aux Fromages
28. Mouff' Tartes
29. Le Jardin des Pâtes
30. La Petite Légume
31. Au Moulin à Vent
32. La Tour d'Argent
33. La Rôtisserie du Beaujolais
34. Inagiku
35. Caveau de la Huchette

★ **Top Picks**

36. Caveau des Oubliettes
37. Café Egyptien
38. Square Tino Rossi
66. Le Vieux Bistro
70. Le Flore en l'Ile
71. Brasserie de l'Ile St-Louis
72. Au Lys d'Argent
73. Mon Vieil Ami
74. La Castafiore
75. Le Fin Gourmet
76. Nos Ancêtres les Gaulois
77. Berthillon
78. La Charlotte de l'Ile

Where to Shop:

39. Librairie Gibert Joseph
41. La Tortue Electrique
42. Diptyque
44. Les Papilles
45. Les Artisans du Rêve:
    Breiz Noway
46. La Tuile à Loup
47. Marché Monge
48. La Quincaillerie
49. Comptoirs Tour d'Argent Art
    de la Table
79. Cacao et Chocolat
80. L'Epicerie
81. Pylones
82. Yamina
83. Le Grain de Sable

Where to Stay:

50. Hôtel Agora St-Germain
51. Hôtel Résidence Henri IV
52. Grand Hôtel St-Michel
53. Hôtel du Panthéon
54. Familia Hôtel
55. Hôtel des Grandes Écoles
56. Hôtel Relais Saint-Jacques
84. Hôtel Saint-Louis
85. Hôtel du Jeu de Paume
86. Hôtel de Lutèce
87. Hôtel des Deux-Îles

LATIN QUARTER

4 to St-Michel;
10 to Cluny-La Sorbonne or Maubert-Mutualité;
7 to Censier-Daubentonn or Place Monge;
7 **10** to Jussieu; **10** to Cardinal Lemoine

● SNAPSHOT ●

The Latin Quarter is the student district where Paris's first university, the Sorbonne, was founded in 1253. At the time, Latin was the language of scholars; thus the area acquired its name. Still buzzing with students and full of different ethnic influences, the Latin Quarter, though commercial and touristy, remains bohemian, vibrant, and full of young people. Although the echoes of the famous 1968 student/worker strike have long faded, the inexpensive shops, ethnic boutiques, avant-garde theatres, and cinemas remain, as do vestiges of much earlier times. Around Boulevard St-Michel, the main street, is a labyrinth of cobblestoned passages, and the rue St-Jacques, an old Roman road, is the precursor of all Parisian streets. The Latin Quarter and its eastern flank, Jussieu, are full of interesting museums, from the magnificent medieval Cluny Museum to the breathtaking Institute of the Arab World with its modern architectural design based on age-old Islamic motifs. Even the Jardin des Plantes, one of Paris's great parks, includes a zoo, botanical school, and the natural history museum and study center, in keeping with the Latin Quarter's centuries-old dedication to culture and learning.

PLACES TO SEE
Landmarks:

At the north end of the busy Boulevard St-Michel, or "Boul'Mich," its nickname, is the **Place St-Michel (1)**, with its ornately sculpted fountain. The site of Paris Commune uprisings in 1871 and student unrest in May 1968, it is now a common meeting point for students. The square borders the river, facing the Pont St-Michel bridge. A stroll along these quays of the Seine is a must: they're filled with the famous bookstalls, the **bouquinistes**. Around the corner from Place St-Michel, along the quay, is **Shakespeare & Co. (2)** *(37 rue de la Bûcherie, 5th, 01-43.25.40.93, www.shakespeareco.org; hours: 10AM–11PM)*, the chaotic but cozy Anglophone bookstore famous for the stream of literati who've flowed through its doors. Nearby, the church of **St-Julien-le-Pauvre (3)** *(1 rue St-Julien-le-Pauvre or 79 rue Galande, 5th, 01-43.29. 09.09)*, now Greek Orthodox, is one of the oldest in Paris. A short, narrow street in this area, the

rue Galande, is synonymous with notorious taverns. A few cobbled streets away, the flamboyant Gothic church **St-Séverin (4)** *(1-3 rue des Prêtres-St-Séverin, 5th; hours: M–F 11AM–7:45PM, Sa 11AM–8PM, Su 9AM–9PM)* flaunts its beauty with spires, balustrades, and gargoyles.

Perhaps the jewel of the Latin Quarter is the **National Museum of the Middle Ages (5)** *(6 pl. Paul-Painlevé, 5th, 01-53.73.78.00, www.musee-moyenage.fr; hours: W–M 9:15AM–5:45PM)*, often referred to by its previous name, the Cluny Museum. A unique combination of Gallo-Roman ruins, baths dating from A.D. 200, and a medieval mansion built by the Abbot of Cluny in 1500, the museum affords the traveler a trip into history, in both its ambience and its collection.

The **Sorbonne (6)** *(47 rue des Écoles, 5th, 01-40.46.2211, www.sorbonne.fr)*, seat of the 13 autonomous University of Paris branches and a world-famous institution of learning, has produced some of the most important intellectuals in history. In the main courtyard, the **Chapel of the Sorbonne** is a monument to Richelieu. Across the street is the research institute **Collège de France (7)** *(11 pl. Marcelin-Berthelot, 5th, 01-44.27.12.11, www.college-de-france.fr; hours: library M–F 10AM–5:30PM)*, founded in 1530.

A few streets south is the **Panthéon (8)** *(pl. du Panthéon, 5th, 01-44.32.18.00; hours: 10AM–6PM)*, originally designed to be an 18th-century neoclassical church, which was built by Louis XV. After surviving a terrible illness, he wanted to give thanks, so he dedicated the building to the patron saint of Paris, Sainte Geneviève; murals telling her story line its interior walls. After the French Revolution, it was turned into a pantheon, the crypt of great figures of France: Voltaire, Jean-Jacques Rousseau, Émile Zola, Victor Hugo, Pierre and Marie Curie, Jean Moulin, and Jean Monnet, father of the European Community, are entombed here.

Other prominent figures have trod the pavement of **Place de la Contrescarpe (9)** *(5th)*. This is where the 16th-century group of writers known as *La Pléiade* used to meet. Ernest Hemingway lived in **39 rue Descartes** when he was an unknown writer, then later with his wife Hadley at **74 rue du Cardinal-Lemoine.**

Today's Parisians teem in the **rue Mouffetard (10)** *(5th)*. It's one of the city's oldest thoroughfares, dating from Roman times. You can still see ancient painted signs on some shops. This pedestrian street is famous today for its open-air markets, especially in **Place Maubert**, **Place Monge**, and the adjacent **rue Daubenton**, home to an upbeat African market. Follow rue Daubenton eastward and you'll arrive at the **Paris Mosque (11)** *(2 bis, pl. du puits de l'Ermite, 5th, 01-45.35.97.33, www. mosquee-de-paris.net; call for hours and guided tours)*. Built in Hispano-Moorish style, the spiritual structure is a splendid creation incorporating decorative tiles, intricately carved lace-like wood screens, and magnificent carpets. The interior patio garden was modeled on the Alhambra in Granada. Its café serves traditional mint tea and delicious pastries. An authentic hammam is open on alternate days to men and women.

Across from the mosque, the **Jardin des Plantes (12)** *(57 rue Cuvier, 5th, 01-40.79.56. 01/54.79, www.mnhn.fr; hours: 7:30AM–7:45PM)*, Paris's botanical garden, boasts ancient trees and remarkable displays of wild and herbaceous plants. It also features a zoo, botanical school, and several galleries of the French **National Museum of Natural History (13)** *(01-40.79.54.79/56.01, www.mnhn.fr; gallery hours vary, call or check Web site for details)*, including galleries of evolution, minerals and geology, and paleontology and comparative anatomy. To the northwest, the **Arènes de Lutèce (14)** *(rue de Navarre, 5th; hours: winter 8AM–5:30PM, summer 8AM–10PM)*, the remains of a Gallo-Roman arena (Romans named Paris "Lutetia"), was probably used for theatrical performances and gladiator fights, a combined use particular to Gaul. Seating 15,000, it was arranged in 35 tiers. Winding northward, you arrive at the **Institute of the Arab World (15)** *(1 rue des Fossées-St-Bernard, 5th, 01-40.51.38.38, www.imarabe. org; hours: Tu–Su 10AM–6PM)*, designed by French architect Jean Nouvel. A breathtaking building that encapsulates the spirit and motifs of traditional Arab architecture using modern materials, this cultural institute and museum was founded in 1980 by France and 20 Arab nations and dedicated to nurturing cultural understanding and cooperation between the Islamic world and the West. The southern façade comprises 1,600 high-tech metal screens; modeled on Moorish screens of carved wood, they filter the sunlight entering the building.

Arts & Entertainment:

For chamber and religious music concerts, **St-Julien-le-Pauvre (3)** *(see also page 112)* is the perfect venue. English-language bookstore **Shakespeare & Co. (2)** *(see also page 112)* hosts poetry readings. The cultural wealth of the Latin Quarter lies in its museums. Besides a superb collection of illuminated manuscripts, sculptures, ceramics, woodcarvings, precious metals, and Gallo-Roman ruins, the **National Museum of the Middle Ages (5)** (also known as Cluny Museum) *(see also page 113)* is home to the famous **Lady with the Unicorn**, a series of six exquisite 15th-century tapestries, the **Gallery of the Kings**, 21 stone heads of the Kings of Judah (13th century), two **Books of Hours** (15th century), and the **Golden Rose of Basel**, a rose sculpted in gold for the Avignon Pope John XXII (14th century). Columns, a pediment relief, and a grandiose dome lend majesty to the façade of the **Panthéon (8)** *(see also page 113)*. Inside, frescoes, statues, and decorative archways are appropriate monuments in this shrine to great personages of French history. On several floors of the magnificent **Institute of the Arab World (15)** *(see also page 115)*, Islamic works of art span the 9th to 19th centuries. The lower level displays art works from the Arab world since 1950: photography, graphic arts, painting, sculpture, and calligraphy. The **National Museum of Natural History (13)** *(see also page 115)* fascinates with its exhibits of humans and animals as well as its mineralogical and gemstone displays. It's famous for its Grand Hall of Evolution.

PLACES TO EAT & DRINK
Where to Eat:

For a long, cozy lunch, **La Fourmi Ailée (16) (€)** *(8 rue du Fouarre, 5th, 01-43.29.40.99, www.parisresto.com; hours: 12PM–12AM)* specializes in tarts; the service is slow but the library-den ambience is charming. **Le Reminet (17) (€-€€)** *(3 rue des Grands-Degrés, 5th, 01-44.07.04.24; hours: Th–M 12PM–2:15PM, 7:30PM–11PM)* was a well-kept secret, but the word is out: the food's memorable; the service delightful. Country flair, Latin Quarter buzz, and a view of Notre-Dame add atmosphere to the classic fare at **L'Atelier Maître Albert (18) (€€)** *(1 rue Maître-Albert, 5th, 01-56.81.30.01, www.ateliermaitrealbert.com; hours: M–W 12PM–2:30PM, 6:30PM–11:30PM, Th–F 12PM–2:30PM, 6:30AM–1AM, Sa 6:30AM–1AM, Su 6:30PM–1:30PM)*. Just north of the Sorbonne, **Le Pré Verre (19) (€€)** *(8 rue Thénard, 5th, 01-43.54.59.47, www.lepreverre.com; hours: Tu–Sa 12PM–2PM, 7:30PM–10:30PM, closed 3 wks Aug)*, one of the newest bistros, charming and casual, whips up inventive dishes with exotic spices, appropriate for the background jazz music. Rub elbows with Left Bank pundits at **Brasserie Balzar (20) (€€)** *(49 rue des Ecoles, 5th, 01-43.54.13.67 www.brasseriebalzar.com; hours: 12PM–11:45PM)*; it hasn't changed much since Sartre and Camus used to drop in, sawdust on the floor and all. **Chantairelle (21) (€€)** *(17 rue de Laplace, 5th, 01-46.33.18.59, www.*

46.33.18.59, www.chantairelle. com; hours: open to 10PM, closed Sa lunch, Su), with its hearty food and rustic décor, is so authentic you might think you were in the Auvergne. Romance mixes with healthy dishes at **Le Berthoud (22)** (€€) *(1 rue Valette, 5th, 01-43.54.38.81; hours: M–F 12PM–11PM, Sa 7PM–1AM, closed Aug 1–15)*.

Restaurants around the Panthéon aren't fussy. Though **Les Fontaines (23)** (€€) *(9 rue Soufflot, 5th, 01-43.26.42.80; hours: open to 11:30PM)* looks shabby, it's a favorite of locals, lowly and elite alike. For home-style French classics, **Le Perraudin (24)** (€€) *(157 rue St-Jacques, 5th, 01-46.33.15.75, www.restaurant-perraudin.com; call for hours)* is the real thing; so typically 1900s, down to the Turkish toilet! **Café de la Nouvelle Mairie (25)** (€-€€) *(19-21 rue des Fossés-St-Jacques, 5th, 01-44.07.04.41; hours: M, W, F 9AM–9PM, Tu, Th 9AM–12AM, closed Aug)* is the perfect café: friendly, relaxing, with a lovely terrace.

Toward **rue Mouffetard (10)**, **Les Cinq Saveurs d'Anada (26)** (€) *(72 rue du Cardinal-Lemoine, 5th, 01-43.29 .58.54; hours: Tu–Su 12PM–2:30PM, 7PM–10:30PM)* serves delicious organic vegetarian dishes. Beware the tourist traps along **rue Mouffetard (10)**. However, rest assured that **L'Assiette aux Fromages (27)** (€) *(25 rue Mouffetard, 5th, 01-43.36.91.59; hours: M–Th 12PM– 2:30PM, 6PM–11:30PM, F, Su 12PM–11:30PM, Sa*

12PM–12AM) isn't one of them. It's all things cheese—fondue, quiches, tarts, raclette—along with great bread and salads. A good cheap eat is **Mouff' Tartes (28)** (€) *(53 rue Mouffetard, 5th, 01-43.37.21.89; call for hours)*, with great quiches and yummy chocolate desserts.

Across from the Jardin des Plantes, the organic pasta at **Le Jardin des Pâtes (29)** (€) *(4 rue Lacépède, 5th, 01-43.31.50.71; hours: open to 11PM)* is delicious: try the chestnut *(châtaigne)* pasta with duck fillet, mushrooms, and cream. Try bargain vegetarian fare at **La Petite Légume (30)** (€) *(36 rue des Boulangers, 5th, 01-40.46.06.85; call for hours)*. On the other end of the spectrum, **Au Moulin à Vent (31)** (€€-€€€) *(20 rue des Fossés-St-Bernard, 5th, 01-43.54.99.37, www.au-moulinavent.com; hours: Tu-F 12PM–2:15PM, 7PM–11PM, Sa 7PM–11PM)* is known for great steaks.

Very expensive, very entrancing, and one of Paris's most fabled restaurants, **La Tour d'Argent (32)** (€€€€) *(17 quai de la Tournelle, 5th, 01-43.54.23.31, www.latourdargent.com; hours: Tu 7:30PM–10PM W-Su 12PM–2PM, 7:30PM–10PM)* is high-class with a fabulous view of Notre-Dame. Its modestly-priced neighbor, **La Rôtisserie du Beaujolais (33)** (€€) *(19 quai de la Tournelle, 5th, 01-43.54.17.47; hours: Tu-Su 12PM–2:15PM, 7:30PM–10:15PM)* has the same view and feeds bustling crowds with less fancy, but tasty, dependable classics. Try fresh seafood, sizzling in front of you on the teppanyaki grill, at **Inagiku (34) (€€€)** *(14 rue de Pontoise, 5th, 01-43.54.70.07; hours: M–Sa 12PM–2PM, 7PM–10:45PM).*

Bars & Nightlife:

Medieval cellars around St-Michel have turned into jazz clubs: **Caveau de la Huchette (35)** *(5 rue de la Huchette, 5th, 01-43.26.65.05, www.caveaudelahuchette.fr; hours: M–W, Su 9:30PM–2:30AM, Th–Sa 9:30PM–dawn)* and **Caveau des Oubliettes (36)** *(25 rue Galande, 5th, 01-46.34.23.09; hours: M–Th, Su 5PM–2AM, F–Sa 5PM–5AM, concerts 10PM daily)* are on the tourist circuit, but they offer good acts. Student nightlife buzzes around **Place de la Contrescarpe (9)** *(see also page 114)*, full of tiny bars and cafés. Check out **Café Egyptien (37)** *(112 rue Mouffetard, 5th, 01-43.31.11.35; hours: Tu–Su 11:30AM–1:30AM)* for Arab music, mint tea, and a midnight nosh. On Sunday evenings from June to October the **Square Tino Rossi (38)** *(5th)* on the banks of the Seine by the Jardin des Plantes fills with hip-shaking rhythm lovers dancing their feet off—rumba, mambo, tango, samba, you name it, they'll swing.

WHERE TO SHOP

The Latin Quarter is full of small shops, mostly catering to students' needs and wallets. Stroll by the **bouquinistes**, the stalls along the quays of the Seine: you'll find new and old books (even first editions), prints, maps, and postcards. **Shakespeare & Co. (2)** *(see also page 112)* is the mecca for English-language book lovers. Shop at Librairie Gibert Joseph (39) *(26, 30, 32, 34 bd. St-Michel, 5th, 01-44.41.88.88, www.gibertjoseph.com; hours: M–Sa 10AM–8PM)* for new and used books, CDs, and notebooks. The treasure trove of toys at La Tortue Electrique (41) *(7 rue Frédéric-Sauton, 5th, 01-43.29 .37.08; hours: M–Sa 2PM–6PM)* will send you back to your childhood, while the divinely scented candles at Diptyque (42) *(34 bd. St-Germain, 5th, 01-43.26.77.44, www.diptyqueparis.com; hours: M–Sa 10AM–7PM)* will transport you back to France when they're burning in your home long after your trip.

Les Papilles (44) *(30 rue Gay-Lussac, 5th, 01-43. 25.20.79; hours: M–Sa open to 10PM, closed 3 wks Aug)* stocks regional French gourmet foods. It is also a restaurant, and a gourmet-lover's delight. Products from Brittany—pea coats, sweaters, striped Breton T-shirts, pottery—are the real thing at Les Artisans du Rêve: Breiz Noway (45) *(33 rue Gay-Lussac, 5th, 01-43.29.47.82).* For shopping or gawking, the open-air markets on **rue Mouffetard (10)** *(see also page 114)* and the African market on **rue Daubenton** afford an authentic Parisian experience. La Tuile à Loup (46) *(35 rue Daubenton, 5th, 01-47.07.28.90; www.latuilealoup.com; hours: M 1–7PM,*

Tu–Sa 10:30AM–7PM) sells regional French table and housewares. Nearby Marché Monge (47) *(pl. Monge, 5th; hours: W, F 7AM–2:30PM, Su 7AM–3PM)*, less touristy, is full of feisty produce hawkers.

Old World door handles and other lovely fixtures can be found at the hardware store La Quincaillerie (48) *(3-4 bd. St-Germain, 5th, 01-46.33.66.71/01-55.42.98.01, www.laquincaillerie.com)*. Comptoirs Tour d'Argent Art de la Table (49) *(2 rue du Cardinal-Lemoine, 5th, 01-46.33.45.58)*, the famous restaurant's shop, sells fine china, crystal, and silverware.

WHERE TO STAY

The rooms at Hôtel Agora St-Germain (50) (€–€€) *(42 rue des Bernardins, 5th, 01-46.34.13.00, www.AgoraSaintGermain.com)* have space, silk wallpaper, marble-tiled bathrooms, and A/C (not a given in non-luxury hotels). Located across a tree-filled square, Hôtel Résidence Henri IV (51) (€–€€) *(50 rue des Bernardins, 5th, 01-44.41.31.81, www.residencehenri4.com)* is quiet and comfortable; kitchenettes and lovely two-room suites are available.

Facing the Sorbonne, Grand Hôtel St-Michel (52) (€€) *(19 rue Cujas, 5th, 01-46.33.33.02, www.grand-hotel-st-michel.com)* has a sophisticated look, with spacious rooms, A/C, and hand-painted furniture. An elegant converted 18th-century town house, the Hôtel du Panthéon (53) (€–€€) *(19 pl. du Panthéon, 5th, 01-43.54. 32.95, www.hoteldupantheon.com)*, with its atrium garden and view of the Panthéon, is tastefully appointed with antique furniture, coordinated fabrics, and framed artwork in high-ceilinged rooms.

Familia Hôtel (54) (€) *(11 rue des Écoles, 5th, 01-43.54. 55.27, www.hotel-paris-familia.com)* is a great deal; exposed stone walls or painted murals coordinate with tapestry wall-hangings. Another bargain is the **Hôtel des Grandes Écoles (55)** (€) *(75 rue du Cardinal-Lemoine, 5th, 01-43.26.79.23, www.hotel-grandes-ecoles.com)*: the terrace overlooks a garden, which will transport you to a peaceful French countryside setting after a long day of city sightseeing.

Hôtel Relais Saint-Jacques (56) (€€-€€€) *(3 rue de l'Abbé-de-l'Épée, 5th, 01-53.73.26.00, toll-free in U.S. 800-44-UTELL, www.relais-saint-jacques.com)* is a boutique hotel inspired by the Loire Valley's châteaux; traditional décor and modern amenities create a luxurious experience.

ÎLE DE LA CITÉ

4 *to Cité or St-Michel;* **1 4 7 14** *to Châtelet*

• SNAPSHOT •

Île de la Cité is where Paris began: around 250 B.C. a tribe of Celtic Gauls, river traders called the Parisii, settled on the island. With the river encircling it like a moat, it was easily defendable. Île de la Cité became the seat of power and the site of a royal palace (now the law courts). Monumental buildings arose: Notre-Dame Cathedral, Sainte-Chapelle, and the Conciergerie. These historical buildings lend majesty to the island and magnificence to the riverfront. Amid the enormity of its power and beauty, the island still contains pockets of smaller-scale charm.

PLACES TO SEE
Landmarks:

The western tip of the island, the tree-lined triangle of the **Square du Vert-Galant (57)** *(1st)*, named after the amorous King Henri IV, is one of the most beautiful areas of Paris. The Seine stretches out on either side; beyond the river, Paris sprawls at your feet. **Pont Neuf** ("New Bridge"), the oldest bridge in Paris, connects the island to the rest of the city. To the east is **Place Dauphine (58)** *(1st)*, another haven of charm and calm. The **Palais de Justice (59)** *(4 bd. du Palais,1st, 01-44.32.50.00; hours: M–F 8:30AM–6:30PM)*, now the law courts, was for centuries the royal palace, until the king moved to the Marais in the 14th century. During the French Revolution, the site became a tribunal. Nestled among the courts, ★SAINTE-CHAPELLE (60) *(4 bd. du Palais, 1st, 01-53.40.60.97, www.monum.fr; hours: Mar–Oct 9:30AM–6PM, Nov–Feb 9AM–5PM)* is among Europe's greatest architectural masterpieces. Famous for its 15 magnificent stained-glass windows depicting more than 1,000 religious scenes, the chapel is characterized by lofty vaulted ceilings. Louis IX built the chapel in 1248 to house Christian relics, including what was purported to be Christ's crown of thorns.

TOP PICK!

To the north is the **Conciergerie (61)** *(2 bd. du Palais/1 quai de l'Horloge, 1st, 01-53.40.60.80, www.monum.fr; hours: Mar–Oct 9:30AM–6PM, Nov–Feb 9AM–5PM)*, the prison made infamous during the Revolution. Marie Antoinette was jailed there until her execution; so were Charlotte Corday, who stabbed Revolutionary leader Marat; and Revolutionary judges Danton and Robespierre. East of the Conciergerie, the famous **Flower and Bird Market (62)** *(pl. Louis-Lépine, 4th; hours: M–Sa 8AM–6PM, Sun 8AM–7PM)* adds a splash of life and color to an area of daunting administrative buildings. Gallo-Roman ruins and vestiges of 2,000-year-old houses are on view in the **Crypte Archéologique (63)** *(1 pl. du Parvis-Notre-Dame, 4th, 01-55.42.50. 10, www.notredamedeparis.fr; hours: Tu–Su 10AM–6PM)*. It is located on

TOP PICK!

the main square of one of Paris's most famous structures, the Gothic cathedral of ★**NOTRE-DAME (64)** *(6 Parvis Notre-Dame de Paris, pl. Jean-Paul II, 4th, 01-42.34.56.10, www.notredamedeparis.fr; hours: M–F 8AM–6:45PM, Sa–Su 8AM–7:15PM).* It took 170 years to build this magnificent cathedral, which was pillaged during the French Revolution and later restored. The heads of the façade's 28 statues of the Kings of Judah remained lost until 1977, when they were unearthed during the construction of a parking lot. They'd

been removed by rebel mobs, who thought the statues to be those of French kings. The originals are now on display in the **National Museum of the Middle Ages (5)** *(see also page 113).* Noted for its flying buttresses, gargoyles (you can

climb up 387 steps in the North Tower to the **Galerie des Chimères** to view these famous carved creatures), and two rose windows of stained glass, the cathedral is a marvel inside and out. Masterpieces of statuary cover the three main doors. Inside, statues, reliefs, paintings, and carved woodwork add to the grandeur. Kings and emperors were crowned beneath these lofty vaults.

Arts & Entertainment:

Notre-Dame (64), **Sainte-Chapelle (60)**, the **Conciergerie (61)**, and the **Crypte Archéologique (63)** are among Paris's most fascinating and oldest treasures. To get an even closer look at historical treasures, visit the **Museum of Notre-Dame de Paris (65)** *(10 rue du Cloître-Notre-Dame, 4th, 01-43.25.42.92; hours: W, Sa–Su 2:30PM–6PM)*, which contains documents, relics, objects, and engravings covering the history of Notre-Dame.

PLACES TO EAT & DRINK
Where to Eat:

Restaurants aren't abundant in this area, so you might be better off eating on Île St-Louis. However, **Le Vieux Bistro (66) (€€)** *(14 rue du Cloître-Notre-Dame, 4th, 01-43.54.18.95; hours: 12PM–10:30PM)*, a classic French bistro, serves great Lyonnais cuisine.

WHERE TO SHOP

The shopping here is basically limited to souvenirs and postcards. Stick to sightseeing and leave shopping for your spin around St-Germain.

WHERE TO STAY

There's not much in the way of lodging in this administrative district. Try Île St-Louis or other nearby areas (Marais, Latin Quarter, and St-Germain).

ÎLE ST-LOUIS

7 *to Pont Marie;* **10** *to Cardinal Lemoine*

• SNAPSHOT •

One of the most beautiful areas of Paris, the Île St-Louis is a haven of serenity and elegance between the bustle and noise of the Left and Right banks. Splendid 17th-century residences line calm streets, and along the romantic quays of the river the views are fabulous. It's a favorite residential area of artists and heiresses—and home to members of the Rothschild family. This is the perfect place to find a moment of repose after days of sightseeing.

PLACES TO SEE
Landmarks:

Stroll the periphery of the island: you'll find not only marvelous views of the city, but also lovely corners, beautiful residences, exquisite wrought-iron balconies, graceful doorways, and superb statuary. Check out the gargoyles that hold up the balcony at **Hôtel Chernizot (67)** *(51 rue St-Louis-en-l'Ile, 4th; closed to public)* and don't miss **Hôtel Lambert (68)** *(rue St-Louis-en-l'Ile at Quai d'Anjou, 4th; closed to public)*, a famous aristocratic 17th-century townhouse. The carved doors of the island church, **Saint-Louis-en-l'Ile (69)** *(19 bis, rue St-Louis-en-l'Ile, 4th, 01-46.34.11.60, www.saintlouisenlile.com; hours: Tu–Su 9AM–12PM, 3PM–7PM)*, are splendid; its clock and tower are also beautiful.

PLACES TO EAT & DRINK
Where to Eat:

With a spectacular view of Notre-Dame and the river, **Le Flore en l'Ile (70) (€€)** *(42 quai d'Orléans, 4th, 01-43.29. 88.27;*

hours: 8AM–2AM) is fabulous for breakfast, tea, desserts; less so for meals. Enjoy a great Alsatian meal at **Brasserie de l'Ile St-Louis (71) (€€)** *(55 quai de Bourbon, 4th, 01-43.54.02.59; hours: M, Tu, F–Su 12PM–12AM, Th 6PM–12AM)*, a favorite of the island's cognoscenti. **Rue St-Louis-en-l'Ile** is the main drag with several appetizing eateries. For a light meal of quiche, salad, *crêpe*, and the like, **Au Lys d'Argent (72) (€)** *(90 rue St-Louis-en-l'Ile, 4th, 01-46.33.56.13; hours: Nov 1–Apr 31 M, Th 12PM–10PM, Tu 12PM–4PM, F–Sa 12PM–10:30PM, Su 11:30AM–6:30PM)* satisfies many tastes and serves brunch daily. The chef at **Mon Vieil Ami (73) (€€)** *(69 rue St-Louis-en-l'Ile, 4th, 01-40.46.01.35, www.mon-vieil-ami.com; hours: W–Su 12PM–2PM, 6:30PM–11PM, closed 3 wks Jan & Aug)* creates imaginative, masterful Alsatian concoctions, lighter than the traditional fare, in a beautiful modern interior. For ethnic variety, **La Castafiore (74) (€-€€)** *(51 rue St-Louis-en-l'Ile, 4th, 01-43.54.78. 62; hours: 12PM–2:30PM, 6:30PM–11PM)* serves wonderful Italian dishes; tiny and sometimes cramped, it's romantically cozy outside rush hours. Robust country classics have local families returning to **Le Fin Gourmet (75) (€€)** *(42 rue St-Louis-en-l'Ile, 4th, 01-43.26.79.27, www.lefingourmet.fr; hours: W–Su 12PM–2:30PM, 7PM–10:30PM)*. Farm food and partying go hand-in-hand at **Nos Ancêtres les Gaulois (76) (€€)** *(39 rue St-Louis-en-l'Ile, 4th, 01-46.33.66.07)*, an all-you-can-eat country inn with long trestle tables. A visit to Paris isn't complete without a stop at the famous ice cream parlor **Berthillon (77) (€)** *(31 rue St-Louis-en-l'Ile, 4th, 01-43.54.31.61, www.berthillon.fr; hours: W–Su 10AM–8PM, closed mid July–early Sept)*: all Parisians know it's the best around. Pastries, chocolates, pure fruit lollipops—**La Charlotte de l'Ile (78) (€)** *(24 rue St-Louis-en-l'Ile, 4th, 01-43.54.25.83, www.la-charlotte.fr; hours: Th–Su 2PM–8PM)* is a sweet lover's delight. The sign in the window says: "Here we sell happiness."

WHERE TO SHOP

Besides restaurants, **rue St-Louis-en-l'Ile** is also the main shopping street. Chocolate pyramids and spicy fillings are just some of the delicacies at **Cacao et Chocolat (79)** *(63 rue St-Louis-en-l'Ile, 4th, 01-46.33.33.33, www.cacaoetchocolat.com; hours: 10:30AM–7:30PM)*. **L'Epicerie (80)** *(51 rue St-Louis-en-l'Ile, 4th, 01-43.25.20.14)* is a great gourmet food gift shop—pick up delicious souvenirs for the folks back home. The funny neckties and suspenders you may have seen at the Pompidou Center are made and sold at **Pylones (81)** *(57 rue St-Louis-en-l'Ile, 4th, 01-46.34.05.02, www.pylones.com)*. Stop in **Yamina (82)** *(56 rue St-Louis-en-l'Ile, 4th, 01-43.29.33.93)* for hand-painted scarves and women's clothing.

Beads galore, cords, and clasps—make your own jewelry masterpieces at **Le Grain de Sable (83)** *(79 rue St-Louis-en-l'Ile, 4th, 01-46.33.67.27, http://legraindesable.fr; hours: W–M 11AM–7PM, Tu 3PM–7PM)* or buy the salespeople's creations; hats are actually the centerpiece of this shop.

WHERE TO STAY

The hotels on **rue St-Louis-en-l'Ile** reflect the romantic charm of the island and its calm, dignified pace. The intimate atmosphere of **Hôtel Saint-Louis (84)** **(€–€€)** *(75 rue St-Louis-en-l'Ile, 4th, 01-46.34.04.80, www.hotelsaintlouis.com)*—with exposed wood beams, tapestry fabrics, antiques, and flowers—makes up for the small rooms. The stunning **Hôtel du Jeu de Paume (85)** **(€€–€€€)** *(54 rue St-Louis-en-l'Ile, 4th, 01-43.26.14.18, www.jeudepaumehotel.com)*, on the grounds of what was once the royal tennis court, has retained the open cross-beamed roof. The rooms, though not sumptuous, have marble bathrooms and comfortable space. Despite small rooms, the beauty of **Hôtel de Lutèce (86)** **(€€)** *(65 rue St-Louis-en-l'Ile, 4th, 01-43.26.23.52, www.paris-hotel-lutece.com)* ensures it's heavily booked. In a beautiful 17th-century mansion, **Hôtel des Deux-Îles (87)** **(€€)** *(59 rue St-Louis-en-l'Ile, 4th, 01-43.26.13.35, www.deuxiles-paris-hotel.com)* enchants, from the lobby's atrium garden to the intimate rooms with bamboo furniture and provincial prints.

chapter 6

ST-GERMAIN

RUE DU BAC

MONTPARNASSE

ST-GERMAIN
RUE DU BAC
MONTPARNASSE

Places to See:

1. St-Germain-des-Prés
2. Hommage to Apollinaire
3. Place de Furstenberg
4. Delacroix Museum
5. Les Deux Magots
6. Café de Flore
7. Brasserie Lipp
8. Rue du Dragon
9. St-Sulpice
10. JARDIN DE LUXEMBOURG ★
11. Palais de Luxembourg
12. Fontaine de Médicis
13. Théâtre National de l'Odéon
14. Le Procope
15. Cour de Rohan
16. Institut de France
17. School of Fine Arts (Beaux-Arts)
18. Théâtre du Vieux Colombier
19. Zadkine Museum
81. MUSÉE D'ORSAY ★
82. Le Bon Marché
83. Musée Maillol
84. La Pagode
116. Tour Montparnasse
117. La Coupole
118. La Closerie des Lilas
119. Rue Campagne-Première
120. Montparnasse Cemetery
121. Catacombs
122. Musée du Montparnasse
123. Fondation Henri Cartier-Bresson
124. Fondation Cartier pour l'Art Contemporain

Places to Eat & Drink:

20. Le Petit St-Benoît
21. La Palette
22. Fish La Boissonnerie
23. Cosi
24. Azabu
25. La Rotisserie d'en Face
26. Ze Kitchen Galerie
27. Mariage Frères
28. Aux Charpentiers
29. Le Petit Vatel
30. Gérard Mulot
31. Le Comptoir du Relais
32. Marco Polo
33. Chez Maître Paul
34. La Bastide Odéon

★ Top Picks

Where to Stay:

ST-GERMAIN

④ to St-Germain-des-Prés, St-Sulpice,
St-Michel, or St-Placide;
⑩ to Mabillon; ④ ⑩ to Odéon;
⑫ to Rennes or Notre-Dame-des-Champs;

• SNAPSHOT •

St-Germain was once the stomping grounds of artists, writers, and intellectuals and the locus of café society. Café life, always important in Paris, has been vital in St-Germain. Verlaine and Rimbaud drank themselves into poetic exaltation here. At the Café de Flore and Les Deux Magots, Sartre, de Beauvoir, and Camus developed their existentialist philosophies, often over coffee and endless cigarettes. Today, St-Germain remains the hub of the French publishing industry, but the writers and artists of the neighborhood are very well heeled. The elegant streets have been taken over by cutting-edge interior design showrooms and art galleries. High-profile fashion designers dot the landscape with their chic, artistic boutiques, making the district one of the finest for shopping. The upscale hip and cultural sophisticates mix with artists and intellectuals in this quarter where literati meet glitterati.

PLACES TO SEE
Landmarks:

The quarter takes its name from the medieval abbey around which it rose: **St-Germain-des-Prés (1)** *(3 pl. St-Germain-des-Prés, 6th, 01-55.42.81.33, www.eglise-sgp.org; hours: M–Sa 8AM–7:45PM, Su 9AM–8PM)* is the oldest church in Paris, dating from 542; it became a Benedictine abbey in the 8th century. It was rebuilt and restored over the centuries; the present church dates from the 11th century. Outside, a Picasso sculpture, **Hommage to Apollinaire (2)** *(rue de l'Abbaye and pl. St-Germain-des-Prés, 6th)*, was created in dedication to the artist's friend, poet Guillaume Apollinaire. One of Paris's most romantic spots is the tiny square **Place de Furstenberg (3)**, a favorite film location. There, the home of 19th-century Romantic painter Eugène Delacroix is now the **Delacroix Museum (4)** *(6 rue de Furstenberg, 6th, 01-44.41.86.50, www.musee-delacroix.fr; hours: W–M 9:30AM–5PM)*.

A result of Baron Haussmann's 19th-century urban planning, the wide, majestic **Blvd. St-Germain** is the main thoroughfare of the district. Replete with café terraces, restaurants, designer boutiques, and book-stores, the segment around the square of St-Germain is prime acreage for celebrity spottings. Some may be having a drink at one of the three most famous café-bars, noted for the writers, musicians, painters, and intellectuals that were regulars. In the 1920s and 1930s Hemingway, The Lost Generation, and the surrealists, followed in the 1950s by existentialists, had their tables at **Les Deux Magots (5)** *(6 pl. St-Germain-des-Prés, 6th, 01-45.48.55.25, www.lesdeuxmagots.com; hours: 7:30AM–1AM)*. Poet Apollinaire held court at **Café de Flore (6)** *(172 bd. St-Germain, 6th, 01-45.48.55.26; hours: 7:30AM–1AM)*, claimed also by Sartre, Camus, and Simone de Beauvoir. Now the haunt of politicians and fashion designers, **Brasserie Lipp (7)** *(151 bd. St-Germain, 6th, 01-45.48.53.91, www.brasserie-lipp.fr; hours: 10AM–1AM)* was once the meeting place for literary luminaries, such as Verlaine, Proust, Gide, and Malraux. Hemingway wrote *A Farewell to Arms* in this café; it has since been classified a historical monument. The next street westward, picturesque **rue du Dragon (8)** *(6th)*, dates from the Middle Ages, and still has 17th- and 18th-century houses.

Explore the narrow streets of the quarter, full of eye-catching boutiques and art galleries, as you make your way southward to splendid **Place St-Sulpice**, dominated by the Fountain of the Four Bishops and pink-flowered chestnut trees. Another popular movie location is **Café de la Mairie**. Construction of the church of **St-Sulpice (9)** *(pl. St-Sulpice, 6th, 01-46.33.21.78, www.paroisse-saint-sulpice-paris.org & www.stsulpice.*

com; hours: 7:30AM-7:30PM) took more than 100 years and is the result of the work of various architects.

The ★**JARDIN DE LUXEMBOURG (10)** *(60 acres encircled by bd. St-Michel, rue de Médicis, rue de Vaugirard, rue Guynemer, and rue August-Comte, 6th, 01-42.34.23.89, www.senat.fr/visite/jardin; hours: times vary; generally, summer 7:30AM–dusk, winter 8:15AM–dusk)* is Paris's most popular park. Formal terraces and wide walkways are adorned with statues of French queens. An octagonal pool, open-air café, puppet theatre, bandstand, and tennis courts are also among the features of this splendid park. The gardens sweep down from the Florentine-style royal palace **Palais de Luxembourg (11)** *(15 rue de Vaugirard, 6th, 01-42.34.20.00, www.senat.fr; call to arrange visits),* now seat of the French Senate. Like the palace, the imposing 17th-century Baroque **Fontaine de Médicis (12)** *(15 rue de Vaugirard, 6th),* to the east, was built for Marie de Médici, Florentine widow of Henri IV.

TOP PICK!

Take rue de Vaugirard east to the **Théâtre National de l'Odéon (13)** *(1 pl. Paul-Claudel, 6th, 01-44.85.40.40, www.theatre-odeon.fr; call for show times),* once the home of the classical theatre company La Comédie Française. To the north, **rue de l'Odéon**, lined with 18th-century houses and shops, is where, at No. 12, Sylvia Beach opened the original Shakespeare & Co. bookshop (1921–1940). Beach was friend and patron of writers such as F. Scott Fitzgerald, Ernest Hemingway, T. S. Eliot, and Ezra Pound. Largely thanks to her, James Joyce's *Ulysses* was first published in English. At the northern end of rue de l'Odéon, on Blvd. St-Germain, is the **Carréfour de l'Odéon**, a square full of cinemas and student cafés—including Starbucks "de Paree"!

Cross Blvd. St-Germain and a few doors in on **rue de l'Ancienne-Comédie** is Le Procope (14) *(13 rue de l'Ancienne-Comédie, 6th, 01-40.46.79.00, www.procope. com; hours: 10:30AM–1AM)*, the world's first café, established in 1686. Voltaire was said to drink 40 cups of coffee there every day; Napoleon was another frequent customer. In the next street over, **Cour du Commerce St-André**, at No. 9, Dr. Guillotin developed his "philanthropic decapitating machine." Around the corner is the charming and quaint 15th-century series of courtyards, Cour de Rohan (15) *(access from rue du Jardinet and bd. St-Germain, 6th)*. The middle one has the only mounting block left in Paris, a *pas-de-mule* from which ladies and portly gentlemen mounted their mules.

Take rue Mazarine all the way to the Seine and the Institut de France (16) *(23 quai de Conti, 6th, 01-44.41.43.32, www.institut-de-france.fr; hours: guided tours by appt, Sa, Su, & holidays)*, its majestic dome visible from afar. Home to five prestigious academies, the institute's most famous group of scholars is the Académie Française, entrusted since 1635 with publishing the definitive French dictionary. Going west along the river, you reach the famous School of Fine Arts (Beaux-Arts) (17) *(13 quai Malaquais, 6th, 01-47.03.50.00, www.ensba.fr/english; hours: Tu–Su 1PM–7PM)*, where artists and architects the world over have been trained.

Arts & Entertainment:

Group tours of the **School of Fine Arts (Beaux-Arts) (17)** *(see also "Places to See", 01-47.03.52.15)* are by appointment only but the exhibition halls and bookstore are open to the public. The **Delacroix Museum (4)** *(see also page 137)* exhibits the painter's passionate canvases in his apartment and garden studio. The architectural mix of the abbey of **St-Germain-des-Prés (1)** *(see also page 137)* is noteworthy: 6th-century marble columns with Romanesque arches beneath Gothic vaults. A surviving original tower houses one of France's oldest belfries. The 17th-century philosopher René Descartes, among other notables, is buried here. If only in size, **St-Sulpice (9)** *(www.stsulpice.com, see also pages 138-139)* would be very impressive; the work of 20 artists makes it unique. In the chapel right of the entrance are three fabulous murals by Delacroix. St-Germain-des-Prés and St-Sulpice also regularly hold concerts.

The **Théâtre du Vieux Colombier (18)** *(21 rue du Vieux-Colombier, 6th, 01-44.39.87.00; call for showtimes and bookings)* one of the venues of the Comédie Française, presents French classics, notably the plays of Molière. The **Théâtre National de l'Odéon (13)** *(see also page 139)* specializes in foreign plays, in their original language. The work of Russian-born sculptor Ossip Zadkine is on display at the **Zadkine Museum (19)** *(100 bis, rue d'Assas, 6th, 01-55.42.77.20, www.zadkine.paris.fr; hours: Tu–Su 10AM–6PM)*, where the artist lived and worked for nearly 40 years. The works cover his artistic development, from Cubism to Expressionism and Abstractionism.

PLACES TO EAT & DRINK
Where to Eat:

St-Germain is so full of good restaurants that it's best to leave the three literary landmark cafés, **Les Deux Magots (5)**, **Café de Flore (6)**, and **Brasserie Lipp (7)** *(see page 138)*, for drinks and people watching. For cheap and retro, the 1901 bistro **Le Petit St-Benoît (20)** (€) *(4 rue St-Benoît, 6th, 01-42.60.27.92, www.petit-st-benoit.com; hours: M–Sa 12PM–2:30PM, 7PM–10:30PM, closed Aug)* is a hoot; Marguerite Duras used to eat at the outdoor tables. Near the Beaux-Arts school and surrounded by art galleries, **La Palette (21)** (€) *(43 rue de Seine, 6th, 01-43.26.68.15; hours: M–Sa 9AM–2AM)* is a neighborhood café full of students, art dealers, and artists. Great fish, wine, and Mediterranean food are part of the appeal of **Fish La Boissonnerie (22)** (€€) *(69 rue de Seine, 6th, 01-43.54.34.69; hours: Tu–Su 12:30PM–10:45PM)*. A best buy is **Cosi (23)** (€) *(54 rue de Seine, 6th, 01-46.33.35.36)*, a fabulous sandwich shop. Japanese teppanyaki specialties, cooked in front of you, are exceptional at **Azabu (24)** (€€) *(3 rue André-Mazet, 6th, 01-46.33.72.05; hours: Tu–Sa 12PM–2PM, 7:30PM–10:30PM, Su 7:30PM–10:30PM)*. The ghosts of Voltaire, Diderot, and Robespierre peer over your shoulder at Paris's oldest café-restaurant, **Le Procope (14)** (€€€) *(see also page 140)*.

Spit-roasted meats are the specialty at **La Rotisserie d'en Face (25)** (€€) *(2 rue Christine, 6th, 01-43.26.40.98, www.jacquescagne.com; hours: M–Th 12PM–2:30PM, 7PM–11PM, F 12PM–2:30PM, 7PM–11:30PM, Sa 7PM–*

11:30PM), frequented by businessmen and the chic alike. Eclectic food in a snazzy minimalist décor with an open, glass-paneled kitchen make a meal at **Ze Kitchen Galerie (26)** (€€–€€€) *(4 rue des Grands-Augustins, 6th, 01-44.32.00.32, www.zekitchengalerie.fr; hours: M–F 12PM–2:30PM, 7PM–11PM, Sa 7PM–11PM)* an artistic experience. For the best afternoon tea or weekend brunch, **Mariage Frères (27)** (€€) *(13 rue des Grands-Augustins, 6th, 01-40.51.82.50, www.mariagefreres.com; hours: 10:30AM–7:30PM)* is a tea mecca.

South of Blvd. St-Germain, a timeless bistro with delicious, simple, classic French food is **Aux Charpentiers (28)** (€€) *(10 rue Mabillon, 6th, 01-43.26.30.05; hours: 12PM–3PM, 7PM–11:30PM)*; it's authentic in both food and décor. Very cheap and funky, that's **Le Petit Vatel (29)** (€) *(5 rue Lobineau, 6th, 01-43.54.28.49; hours: Tu–Sa 12PM–2:30PM, 7PM–10:30PM)*. Delightful picnic food and scrumptious pastries make up for the window-counter seating at the bakery **Gérard Mulot (30)** (€) *(76 rue de Seine, 6th, 01-43.26.85.77, www.gerard-mulot.com; hours: Th–Tu 7AM–8PM, closed 4 wks July–Aug)*.

To experience a 1930s bistro, have lunch at **Le Comptoir du Relais (31)** (€€) *(9 Carrefour de l'Odéon, 6th, 01-44.27.07.97; hours: brasserie M–F 12PM–10:30PM, Sa–Su 12PM–6PM; restaurant M–F 8:30PM–10:30PM, for weeknight dinner reserve 3 mon in advance)*: it's small, has the requisite mirrored walls, and serves great grilled tuna, lamb, and rich cheeses. **Marco Polo (32)** (€€) *(8 rue de Condé, 6th, 01-43.26.79.63; hours: M–Sa 12PM–2:15PM, 7:15PM–11:15PM, Su 7:15PM–11:15PM)* is a popular Italian eatery. Delicious, not-to-be-missed: that's what they say about **Chez Maître Paul (33)** (€€) *(12 rue Monsieur-le-Prince, 6th, 01-43.54.74.59, www.chezmaitrepaul.fr; hours: 12PM–2:30PM, 7PM–10:30PM, closed some days in July–Aug)*, a refined bistro.

Near the Luxembourg Gardens, **La Bastide Odéon (34)** (€€) *(7 rue Corneille, 6th, 01-43.26.03.65, www.bastide-odeon.com; hours: Tu–Sa 12:15PM–2PM, 7:30PM–10:30PM)* offers memorable Provençal cooking in a cheerful setting. **Kiwi Corner (35)** (€–€€) *(25 rue Servandoni, 6th, 01-46.33.12.06, www.kiwicorner.fr; hours: M–W 12PM–3PM, 7PM–9:30PM, Th–Sa 12PM–3PM, 7PM–9:15PM, 9:30PM–11:30PM, Su brunch 12PM–3:30PM)* offers a taste of Australia and New Zealand. Try the crab cakes with wasabi mayo, kangaroo steak in BBQ sauce, or kingfish and scallops in citrus/ginger sauce. At the gem **Le Carré de Marguerite (36)** (€€) *(87 rue d'Assas, 6th, 01-43.26.33.61, www.lecarredemarguerite.fr; open Tu–F 12PM–2PM, 8PM–10PM, Sa 8PM–10PM)* chef Gilles Choukroun is fabulously innovative with a delicious blend of Nouvelle and North African cuisine in a casual, contemporary, exotic décor; and the Afro-Cuban music is great.

Bars & Nightlife:

Miles Davis made jazz history at **Le Bilboquet (37)** *(13 rue St-Benoît, 6th, 01-45.48.81.84; hours: jazz daily 9:30PM–1:30AM; dinner M–Sa 8PM–2AM)*, now an ornate Belle Époque dinner-jazz venue. Occasionally big names play there and movie stars hobnob; call to see if dinner is mandatory. A young crowd gathers at the Canadian sports bar and grill **The Moose (38)** *(16 rue des Quatre-Vents, 6th, 01-46.33.77.00, www.moosehead paris.com, hours: M–F 4PM–2AM, Sa–Su 11AM–2AM)*; it airs sports events and U.S. TV shows. The wine bar **La Crémerie Caves Miard (39)** *(9 rue des Quatre-Vents, 6th, 01-43.54.99.30; hours: Tu–Sa 10AM–10PM)*, formerly a dairy shop, is adorably tiny, with a unique selection of wines.

WHERE TO SHOP

From "hiply" conservative to avant-garde, St-Germain offers some of the best shopping in Paris. Style is the byword here, from clothes to art, furniture, and books. Antique shops, art galleries, and eclectic interior designers abound in **rue Mazarine, rue Jacob, rue de Seine, rue Bonaparte**, and **rue des Saint-Pères**. The French design furniture at **Alexandre Biaggi (41)** *(14 rue de Seine, 6th, 01-44.07.34.73)* covers all the great names of the 1930s to 1950s. Clothing at **Loft Design by (42)** *(56 rue de Rennes, 6th, 01-45.44.88.99, www.loftdesign by.com)* is fashionably black or gray. The picturesque **open-air food market** at rue de Buci (43) *(on rue de Seine and rue de Buci, from bd. St-Germain, 6th, daily except Mondays)* finds Parisians engaged in a favorite pastime. Exceptional furniture and sculpture from the 1940s to the 1970s are the crowning glory of Galerie Yves Gastou (44) *(12 rue Bonaparte, 6th, 01-53.73.00.10, www. galerieyvesgastou.com).* La Maison Ivre (45) *(38 rue Jacob, 6th, 01-42.60.01.85)* stocks beautiful ceramics and linens from Provence. Unusual antiques at Yveline (46) *(4 rue Furstenberg, 6th, 01-43.26.56.91)* delight even the most experienced shopper.

Besides its beauty, **Blvd. St-Germain** is lined with great shops. The famous bookstore La Hune (47) *(170 bd. St-Germain, 6th, 01-45.48.35.85; hours: M–Sa 10AM–11:45PM, Su 11AM–7:45PM)* is known for its art, design, photography, and architecture books (in English and French), while its collection of fiction and critical works can keep you browsing 'til closing time at midnight. Façonnable (48) *(174 bd. St-Germain, 6th, 01-40.49.02.47, www.faconnable.com),* preppie with a fashionable French flair, is overwhelmingly men's wear but also has a line for women. Parisian chic means comfortable skinny knits for women and casual elegance for men at Sonia Rykiel (49) *(women: 175 bd. St-Germain, 6th, 01-49.54.60.60; men: 194 bd. St-Germain, 6th, 01-49.54.60.96; www.soniarykiel.fr).* Rykiel Woman (50) *(6 rue de Grenelle, 6th, 01-49.54.66.21)* includes a range of intimate adult toys and accessories. Next door *(No. 4)* is the designer's line of children's fashions. For the Rykiel look that won't break the bank, head for **Sonia by Sonia Rykiel** *(59 rue des Saints-Pères, 6th, 01-49.54.61.00)*.

Lovely narrow streets south of Blvd. St-Germain—**rue du Four, rue de Rennes, rue Bonaparte, rue du Vieux-Colombier**, and the myriad criss-crossing streets—reveal a cornucopia of fashion designers and art galleries. Pastry chef extraordinaire Pierre Hermé (51) *(72 rue Bonaparte, 6th, 01-43.54.47.77, www.pierreherme.com)* treats his work like high-end fashion, by creating seasonal "collections." Those in the know line up for his creations. Harel (60) *(7 rue de Tournon, 6th, 01-43.54.16.16)* is known for its lovely handmade shoes. The glamorous, expensive lingerie at Sabbia Rosa (52) *(71-73 rue des Sts-Pères, 6th, 01-45.48.88.37)* is worthy of its French starlet clientele; items can be made to order. Shops along **rue du Cherche-Midi** are especially inviting. Robert Clergerie (54) *(5 rue du Cherche-Midi, 6th, 01-45.48.75.47, www.robert clergerie.fr)* offers beauty and comfort in practical daytime shoes. A few doors away Poilâne (55) *(8 rue du Cherche-Midi, 6th, 01-45.48.42.59, www.poilane.com; hours: M–Sa 7:15AM–8:15PM)* continues to make its famous bread, along with other bakery delights. On Sunday mornings *(9AM–1PM)* the organic market Marché Biologique (56) *(bd. Raspail between rue du Cherche-Midi and rue de Rennes, 6th; hours: organic market Su 9AM– 1:30PM; regular market Tu,*

F 7AM–2:30PM) is full of incredibly beautiful and delicious produce and products.

Leather designs in vibrant colors are the signature at **Peggy Huyn Kinh (57)** *(11 rue Coëtlogon, 6th, 01-42.84.83.82, www.phk.fr).* **Longchamp (58)** *(21 rue du Vieux-Colombier, 6th, 01-42.22.74.75, www.longchamp.com)* doesn't stop at great handbags; its luggage collection is just as wonderful. **Vanessa Bruno (59)** *(25 rue St-Sulpice, 6th, 01-43.54.41.04, www.vanessabruno.com)* designs—flattering, feminine, and sporty—are extremely popular.

Master *chocolatier* **Christian Constant (61)** *(37 rue d'Assas, 6th, 01-53.63.15.15, www.christian constant.com; hours: M–F 8:30AM–9PM, Sa–Su 8:30AM–8:30PM)* seeks inspiration around the globe for his creations. Way cool fashion for women and men at **APC (62)** *(38 rue Madame, 6th, 01-42.22.12.77, www.apc.fr),* designed by Jean Touitou, has followers all over Paris *(past-season items are discounted at 45 rue Madame, 6th).* Exceptional architecture and design books are the focus at **Librairie le Moniteur (63)** *(7 pl. de l'Odéon, 6th, 01-44.41.15.75, www.librairiedumoniteur.com).* The jewelry at **Galerie Hélène Porée (64)** *(1 rue de l'Odéon, 6th, 01-43.54.17.00, www.galerie-helene-poree.fr; hours: 11AM–1PM, 2PM–7PM)* is truly wearable art. **Le Mouton à Cinq Pattes (65)** *(138 bd. St-Germain, 6th, 01-*

43.26.49.25, www.mouton-a-cinq-pattes.info) unearths vintage designer clothes and last season's numbers. The store has two other outlets *(8 & 18 rue Saint-Placide, 6th, 01-45.48.86.26 and 01-42.84.25.11).*

WHERE TO STAY

Famous 19th-century guests created delicious scandals at L'Hôtel (66) (€€€-€€€€) *(13 rue des Beaux-Arts, 6th, 01-44.41.99.00, www.l-hotel.com)*; Oscar Wilde died there and music-hall star Mistinguett was a regular. Today, the luxurious hotel frequented by show-biz celebrities, is dramatic, flamboyant, and wonderful. Charming and well-managed, Hôtel du Danube Saint-Germain (67) (€-€€) *(58 rue Jacob, 6th, 01-42.60.34.70, www.hoteldanube.fr)* has spacious rooms in a mix of styles. A walled garden, wood-paneled rooms, and many small details make a stay at Hôtel St-Germain-des-Prés (68) (€€-€€€) *(36 rue Bonaparte, 6th, 01-43.26.00.19, www.hotel-paris-saint-germain.com)* special.

Romantic, small, and charming Hôtel d'Angleterre (69) (€-€€) *(44 rue Jacob, 6th, 01-42.60.34.72, www.hoteldangleterre.com)* welcomes guests warmly. A 17th-century town house with beamed ceilings and Aubusson tapestries, Hôtel d'Aubusson (70) (€€€) *(33 rue Dauphine, 6th, 01-43.29. 43.43, www.hoteldaubusson.com)* is beautifully decorated. Dignified but not stuffy, Au Manoir St-Germain-des-Prés (71) (€€) *(153 bd.*

St-Germain, 6th, 01-42.22.21.65, toll-free in U.S.& Canada 800-528-1234, www.paris-hotels-charm.com) is charming and comfortable, with large bedrooms and airy common rooms. The **Artus Hôtel (72)** (€€-€€€) (*34 rue de Buci, 6th, 01-43.29.07.20, www.artushotel.com*), with its zebra-patterned armchairs, stone fountain, and doors hand-painted by local artists, is unusual, imaginative, and chic, with simple, well-designed rooms.

Oriental rugs, tapestries, brocades, and arbors of blooming plants enhance the thick beams and stone walls of **Grand Hôtel de l'Univers (73)** (€-€€€) (*6 rue Grégoire-de-Tours, 6th, 01-43.29.37.00, toll-free in U.S. 800-528-1234, www.hotel-paris-univers.com*). Beautiful **Le Madison Hôtel (74)** (€€-€€€) (*143 bd. St-Germain, 6th, 01-40.51.60.00, www.hotel-madison.com*)—its sitting areas adorned with tapestries and antiques—combines modern amenities in the rooms with conventional furnishings, evoking the gracious charm of old inns. A great location and cheap prices make up for the small, worn-out rooms in the clean, unpretentious **Welcome Hôtel (75)** (€) (*66 rue de Seine, 6th, 01-46.34.24.80, www.hotelwelcomeparis.com*).

Oak beams, stone walls, Aubusson tapestries, and an abundance of fresh flowers give **Hôtel Left Bank St-Germain (76)** (€-€€€) (*9 rue de l'Ancienne-Comédie, 6th, 01-43.54.01.70, toll-free in U.S. & Canada 800-528-1234,*

www.paris-hotels-charm.com) much of its allure; the standard-size rooms are comfortable. Gracious common areas in the appealing **Hôtel de Fleurie (77)** (€€-€€€) *(32 rue Grégoire-de-Tours, 6th, 01-53.73.70.00, www.hotel-de-fleurie.fr)* are matched by

rooms with a good layout and marble bathrooms. Location is the advantage of **Atlantis St-Germain-des-Prés (78)** (€€) *(4 rue du Vieux-Colombier, 6th, 01-45.48.31.81, www.hotelatlantis.com)*, across from St-Sulpice Church; clean rooms are decorated in a mix of Art Deco and traditional French. Nearby, at spectacular **Hôtel de l'Abbaye (79)** (€€-€€€) *(10 rue Cassette, 6th, 01-45.44.38.11, www.hotelabbaye.com)*, once a 16th- and 17th-century convent, the cobblestone courtyard leads to a splendid reception and salon, while top-floor suites offer fireplaces, arched ceilings, and rooftop views. A super-cheap sleep across from the Luxembourg Gardens, **Pension Les Marronniers (80)** (€) *(78 rue d'Assas, 6th, 01-43.26.37.71, www.pension-marronniers.com)* is a fast-disappearing species, a pension with breakfast and dinner included; most bedrooms, basic and clean, share bathrooms.

⑫ *to Solférino or rue du Bac;* ⑩ ⑫ *to Sèvres-Babylone*

• SNAPSHOT •

The rue du Bac, an area of high-end design and fashion, is a slice of the Left Bank snuggled between sophisticated, hip St-Germain and refined, aristocratic Invalides. Elegant residential facades give a more sedate air to the neighborhood, though boutiques and restaurants claim the cream of French architectural and interior design—with names such as Philippe Starck, Andrée Putman, and Christian Biecher. The spectacular Musée d'Orsay is one of the highlights of this quarter.

PLACES TO SEE
Landmarks:

The **Quai Voltaire** has great river views of Concorde, the Tuileries Gardens, and the Louvre. Famous residents of the street include: Louise de Kéroualle, spy for Louis XIV, at Nos. 3-5; composers Richard Wagner and Jean Sibelius, poet Charles Baudelaire, and writer-pundit Oscar Wilde at No. 19; while No. 27 is where philosopher Voltaire died. Further east is the superb ★**MUSÉE D'ORSAY (81)** *(1 rue de la Légion-d'Honneur at Quai Anatole France, 7th, 01-40.49.48.14, www.musee-orsay.fr; hours: Tu–W, F–Su 9:30AM–6PM, Th 9:30AM–9:45PM).* Dedicated to artistic creation from 1848 to 1914, it includes works by Carpeaux, Cézanne, Daumier,

TOP PICK!

Degas, Delacroix, Gauguin, Manet, Monet, Renoir, Rodin, and van Gogh, among others. The collection of Impressionist art belonging to the Jeu de Paume before it closed in 1986 is now housed here. Once a train station, the building itself is as magnificent as the art it

houses. Retaining much of the original architecture and ironwork, the museum's interior is lofty, airy, and spacious, the openness enhanced by wide exhibition spaces on multiple levels.

Rue du Bac is a classy street lined with elegant boutiques. The buildings and storefronts, many designed by France's top interior decorators, are as fascinating to look at as the wares inside. At the southern end of rue du Bac, you come to **Le Bon Marché (82)** *(24 rue de Sèvres, 7th, 01-44.39.80.00, www.lebonmarche.fr; hours: M–W, F 9:30AM–7PM, Th 10AM–9PM, Sa 9:30AM–8PM)*, Paris's first department store. Designed by Gustave Eiffel, creator of the Eiffel Tower, the *fin-de-siècle* and Art Deco decoration of this landmark inspire some of the awe that Paris wins and deserves.

Arts & Entertainment:

The **Musée d'Orsay (81)** *(see also page 152)* houses a stunning collection of Impressionist paintings, Art Nouveau pieces, mid-to-late-19th-century works, and late-19th-century through early-20th-century paintings and sculptures. Architectural reproductions cover a wide range of styles represented in Parisian buildings. The **Musée Maillol (83)** *(59-61 rue de Grenelle, 7th, 01-42.22.59.58, www.museemaillol.com; hours: W–M 11AM–6PM)* contains the artist's remarkable voluptuous sculptures and his other works, from drawings and engravings to paintings. It also includes works of artists, such as Rodin, Picasso, and Cézanne. A hot Parisian venue for alternative international films, **La Pagode (84)** *(57 bis, rue de Babylone, 7th, 01-45.55.48.48; call for show times)* escaped demolition in the 1970s as a result of the efforts by film director Louis Malle.

PLACES TO EAT & DRINK
Where to Eat:

If the jet-set bistro **Le Voltaire (85)** *(€€€-€€€€)* *(27 Quai Voltaire, 7th, 01-42.61.17.49; hours: Tu–Sa 12:30PM–2:30PM, 7:30PM–10:30PM, closed Aug)* makes your head spin, the much more affordable café next door, "Le Petit Voltaire," serves delicious soups and omelettes. The museum restaurant, **Restaurant du Musée d'Orsay (86)** *(€-€€)* *(1 rue du Légion d'Honneur, 7th, 01-45.49.47.03, www.musee-orsay.fr; hours: Tu–W, F–Su 11:45AM–2:45PM, 3:30PM–5:30PM, Th 11:45AM–2:45PM, 7PM–9:30PM)*

offers lunch and tea in a spectacular setting with a magnificent view. For a light meal, the tearoom **Les Nuits des Thés (87)** *(€)* *(22 rue de Beaune, 7th, 01-*

47.03.92.07, www.lesnuitsdesthes.com; hours: M–Sa 11AM–7PM, Su 3:30PM–7PM) is pleasant and relaxing. The old-fashioned refinement of the quarter's dignified upper crust is reflected in the décor and menu at **La Calèche (88)** (€€) *(8 rue de Lille, 7th, 01-42.60.24.76; hours: M–Sa open to 10:30PM, closed 2 wks Aug)*.

With a no-reservations policy, it's a wait getting into the culinary hot spot **L'Atelier de Joël Robuchon (89)** (€€€€) *(5 rue de Montalembert, 7th, 01-42.22.56.56, www.joel-robuchon.com; hours: 11:30AM– 3:30PM, 6:30PM–12AM)*, but it's worth it: you sit at U-shaped counters and taste tapas—like morsels of food for the gods. The soufflés are exceptional at **La Cigale Récamier (90)** (€€) *(4 rue Récamier, 7th, 01-45.48.86.58; hours: open to 11PM, closed Su)*. French standards prepared in large portions by the motherly owner of **Au Babylone (91)** (€) *(13 rue de Babylone, 7th, 01-45.48.72.13; hours: M–Sa lunch only, closed Aug)* satisfy anyone's nostalgia for typical French lunches of the past.

Audacious, light, clever, out of this world—these are some of the ways people describe the surprising, delicious creations of chef-owner Claude Colliot at **Le Bamboche (92)** (€€–€€€) *(15 rue de Babylone, 7th, 01-45.49.14.40, www.lebamboche.com; hours: M–Sa 12PM–2:30PM, 7PM–11PM, Su 7PM–11PM, book ahead)*. The in-store café at Le Bon Marché, **Delicabar (93)**

01-42.22.10.12, www.delicabar.fr; hours: M–W, F 9:30AM–7PM, Th 10AM–9PM, Sa 9:30AM–8PM), designed by Claudio Colucci and featuring an open courtyard terrace, serves sweet and savory delicacies: try the delectable chocolate *foie gras*!

Reserve in advance to get into a place everyone raves about: **L'Epi Dupin (94) (€€)** *(11 rue Dupin, 6th, 01-42.22.64.56, www.epidupin.com; hours: M 7PM–10:30PM, Tu–F 12PM–2:30PM, 7PM–10:30PM, closed Aug)*, near the Bon Marché, serves refined versions of bistro classics in a friendly atmosphere (though it gets hectic at rush hours, the consensus is it's worth it). The *crêperie* **Le Goémon (95) (€)** *(11 rue Oudinot, 7th, 01-42.73.35.17; hours: M–W 12PM–2PM, 7PM–9:30PM, Th–F 7PM–9:30PM)* is a hidden treasure. Another fabulous cheap eat is **Chez Germaine (96) (€)** *(30 rue Pierre-*

Leroux, 7th, 01-42.73.28.34; hours: M–F 12PM–2:15PM, 7PM–10PM, Sa 12PM–2:15PM, closed Aug), whose homespun food is rich and authentic.

Bars & Nightlife:
This quiet, refined quarter tends to close shop early. St-Germain is more conducive to nightlife.

WHERE TO SHOP
Take to the streets and browse the many *antiquaires* in this quarter. The shops of **Carré Rive Gauche (97)** *(bordered by quai Voltaire, rue des St-Pères, rue de l'Université, and rue du Bac)*, an association of antique dealers, carry quality

items from the grandiose to the rustic. The 1940s look is the thing at **Corinne Sarrut (99)** *(4 rue du Pré-aux-Clercs, 7th, 01-42.61.71.60)*, who designed Audrey Tautou's costumes for the film *Amélie*. Connoisseurs know the chocolates magnificently displayed at **Debauve & Gallais (100)** *(30 rue des Sts-Pères, 7th, 01-45.48.54.67, www. debauve-et-gallais.com)* are among the most divine; you can order online from abroad. **Alain Mikli (101)** *(74 rue des Sts-Pères, 7th, 01-45.49.40.00, www.mikli.fr)* carries the designer's signature eyeglasses as well as his funky, futuristic ready-to-wear collection and handbags. Exquisite chocolates at **Richart (102)** *(258 bd. St-Germain, 7th, 01-45.55.66.00, www.richart.com)* come with tips on chocolate appreciation.

The signature cuts and finishes of **Yohji Yamamoto (103)** *(22 rue de Sèvres, 7th, 01-45.44.29.32)* are inspired by the kimono. Nine perfume-makers have created the unique, complex scents at **Editions de Parfums Frédéric Malle (104)** *(37 rue de Grenelle, 7th, 01-45.05.39.02, www.editionsdeparfums.com)*.

The famous French interior designer **Christian Liaigre (105)** *(42 rue du Bac, 7th, 01-53.63.33.66, www. christian-liaigre.fr)* has decorated hotels, stores, and restaurants in Paris and New York; here his furniture and lighting creations are sold. For four generations **Ryst Dupeyron (106)** *(79 rue du Bac, 7th, 01-45.48.80.93, www.ryst-dupeyron.com)* has sold *armagnac* and

45.48.80.93, www.ryst-dupeyron.com) has sold *armagnac* and fine spirits, with bottled treasures dating from 1868.

Le Bon Marché (82) *(see also page 153)* is the most chic of all Parisian department stores. It offers the latest in designer fashions for both women and men, as well as its own (less expensive) brand. The food hall, **La Grande Épicerie**, presents luscious displays in a grand setting.

WHERE TO STAY

If your priority is peace and quiet, this sedate neighborhood might be just the thing. Understated, tasteful rooms at **Hôtel d'Orsay (107)** (€€-€€€) *(93 rue de Lille, 7th, 01-47.05.85.54, www.esprit-de-france.com)* are warmly decorated and reasonably priced. Clean and quiet, **Hôtel Bersoly's St-Germain (108)** (€-€€) *(28 rue de Lille, 7th, 01-42.60.73.79, www.bersolyshotel.com)* offers basic amenities. In a 17th-century building with original cross beams and stone walls, the small, charming **Hôtel Verneuil (109)** (€-€€) *(8 rue de Verneuil, 7th, 01-42.60. 82.14, www.hotelverneuil.com)* is run by an art collector who has made it her mission to make you feel like a guest in her home.

The budget-conscious can still spend the night in this tiny quarter: though it hasn't seen renovations in decades, **Hôtel de l'Université (110)** (€-€€) *(22 rue de l'Université, 7th, 01-42.61.09.39, www.hoteluniversite. com)* does offer huge, comfortable rooms with fraying vintage furnishings; two rooms are *sans* toilet. An arty crowd appreciates the Art Deco lobby with its elephant and panther statues, as well as the jazz bar at **Hôtel Lenox St-Germain (111)** (€-€€) *(9 rue de l'Université, 7th, 01-42.96. 10.95, www.lenoxsaintgermain.com)*; rooms are more classically furnished.

Rooms at the elegant **Le Montalembert (112)** (€€€-€€€€) *(3 rue Montalembert, 7th, 01-45.49.68.68, www.mon talembert.com)* vary enormously in style, from contemporary chic to Louis-Philippe pomp. Simple, smart, and well-designed, **Hôtel St. Thomas d'Aquin (113)** (€) *(3 rue Pré-aux-Clercs, 7th, 01-42.61. 01.22, www.hotel-st-thomas-daquin.com)* is an excellent deal; therefore, usually booked.

Sumptuous and distinguished, the luxurious Regency-styled **Hôtel Duc de Saint-Simon (114)** (€€-€€€) *(14 rue de St-Simon, 7th, 01-44.39.20.20, www.hotelducdesaint simon.com)* caters to a discerning clientele. At the grand Left Bank establishment **Hôtel Lutétia (115)** (€€€) *(45 bd. Raspail, 6th, 01-49.54.46.46, toll-free from U.S. & Canada 1-800-888-4747, www.lutetia-paris.com)*, the rooms are plush, the hallways graced with statues, and the service impeccable.

MONTPARNASSE

⓸ ⓺ ⑫ ⑬ *to Montparnasse-Bienvenüe;* ⓸ *to Vavin;*
⓺ *to Edgar Quinet;* ⑬ *to Gaîté;*
⓸ ⓺ *to Raspail or Denfert-Rochereau*

● SNAPSHOT ●

Montparnasse was once the neighborhood of illustrious artists: Picasso, Léger, Soutine, Braque, Modigliani, Chagall, Zadkine, and Man Ray lived there, as did writers Gertrude Stein, Henry Miller, and Ezra Pound. Between the two World Wars it was the symbol of modernity, a

hotbed of intellectual and artistic creativity. Those days are long gone. The first Parisian sky-scraper, the Tour Montparnasse, caused horror in the 1970s, resulting in changes in building regulations. The area has unfortu-

nately suffered from tragic urban development policies, but it's worth a trip just to visit the haunts of some of the 20th century's great cultural and artistic figures.

PLACES TO SEE
Landmarks:

The **Tour Montparnasse (116)** *(33 ave. du Maine, 15th, www.tourmontparnasse56.com; hours: Apr–Sep 9:30 AM–11:30PM; Oct–Mar Su–Th 9:30AM–10:30PM, F–Sa 9:30AM–11PM)* was the biggest office building in Europe when it was built in 1973. An observation deck on the

56th floor provides good views of the city, as does the rooftop terrace. Below, the café-restaurant **La Coupole (117)** (*102 bd. du Montparnasse, 14th, 01-43.20.14.20, www.flobrasseries.com or www.lacoupoleparis.com; hours: Su–Th 12PM–1AM, F–Sa 12PM–1:30AM; breakfast 8:30AM–10:30AM*) has had a famous artistic clientele, including Jean-Paul Sartre, Josephine Baker, and Roman Polanski. **La Closerie des Lilas (118)** (*171 bd. du Montparnasse, 14th, 01-40.51.34.50, www.closeriedeslilas.fr; hours: 12PM–1AM*) was the favorite café-bar of Hemingway, F. Scott Fitzgerald, Lenin, and Trotsky. The café is practically a character in Hemingway's novel *The Sun Also Rises*, which he wrote on the terrace in six weeks. Art Deco buildings ornament **rue Campagne-Première (119)** (*14th*), the street where many artists lived between the two World Wars; among them, Picasso, Kandinsky, and Joan Miró. Modigliani, suffering from tuberculosis and opium addiction, lived in No. 3.

The **Montparnasse Cemetery (120)** (*3 bd. Edgar-Quinet, 14th, 01-44.10.86.50; hours: Mar16–Nov 5 M–F 8AM–6PM, Sa 8:30AM–6PM, Su 9AM–6PM; Nov 6–Mar 15 M–F 8AM–5:30PM, Sa 8:30AM–5:30PM, Su 9:30AM–5:30PM*), commissioned by Napoleon, is the resting place of many famous writers and artists. Among them are: Samuel Beckett, Charles Baudelaire, Jean-Paul Sartre, Simone de Beauvoir, Guy de Maupassant, Tristan Tzara, Eugene Ionesco, Constantin Brancusi, Frédéric Bartholdi (sculptor of the Statue of Liberty), Man Ray, Chaïm Soutine, Jean Seberg, Camille Saint-Saëns, André Citroën, Serge Gainsbourg, and Henri Laurens.

Beneath the streets of Paris runs a 3,000-km network of tunnels (nearly 2,000 miles). During World War II the passages were used by the Resistance; in 1968, by demonstrating students evading the cops. In one of these spaces, just before the French Revolution, the bones of six million Parisians were transferred by wheelbarrow from overcrowded cemeteries within the city and dumped into the **Catacombs (121)** *(1 ave. Colonel Henri-Rol-Tanguy, 14th, www.catacombes-de-paris.fr; hours: Tu–Su 9:30AM–5PM, ticket office closes 4PM)*. During the Reign of Terror, more bodies were dumped there. The bones of Marat, Robespierre, and other French citizens are packed in layer upon layer of skulls and bones, all on public display some 25 yards below the streets of the city.

Arts & Entertainment:

The **Musée du Montparnasse (122)** *(21 ave. du Maine, 15th, 01-42.22.91.96, www.museedumontparnasse.net; hours: Tu–Su 12:30PM–7PM)* captures the ethos of the early 20th century's bohemian quarter in what used to be a hangout for Montparnasse artists such as Picasso, Modigliani, and Chagall. The **Fondation Henri Cartier-Bresson (123)** *(2 impasse Lebouis, 14th, 01-56.80.27.00, www.henricartierbresson.org; hours: W 1PM–8:30PM; Th, F, Su 1PM–6:30PM; Sa 11AM–6:45PM)* is a museum dedicated to the works of the great French photographer. The **Fondation Cartier pour l'Art Contemporain (124)** *(261 bd. Raspail, 14th, 01-42.18.56.50, www.fondation. cartier.com; hours: Tu 11AM–10PM, W–Su 11AM–8PM)*, a center for contemporary art, theatre, music, and dance, is housed in a spectacular glass building designed by Jean Nouvel. Depending on how the sun hits it, passersby can either catch a glimpse of the exhibits inside, or see reflections of the busy urban surroundings along the boulevard.

PLACES TO EAT & DRINK
Where to Eat:

Montparnasse was a social hub for early 20th-century artists and writers. It was common to sight the likes of Picasso, Modigliani, Cocteau, Apollinaire, Hemingway, F. Scott Fitzgerald, and many others along Boulevard du Montparnasse—especially in the two favorite café-bar-restaurants. The literati are long gone, but the restaurants remain. You can only imagine discussing feminism with Simone de Beauvoir over an *apéritif* at the Art Deco-styled **La Coupole (117)** (€€) *(102 bd. du Montparnasse, 14th, 01-43.20.14.20, www.lacoupoleparis.com or www.florbrasseries.com; hours: 8:30AM–10:30AM, Su–Th 12PM–1AM, F–Sa 12PM–1:30AM)*. Today, one goes there because of its illustrious history, not for the food; drinks will do the trick just as well. On the other hand, **Le Dôme (125)** (€€€) *(108 bd. du Montparnasse, 14th, 01-43.35. 25.81; hours: 12PM–3PM, 7PM–12:30AM, closed Su–M in Aug)*, that other Montparnasse institution, offers fabulous fish and seafood in an equally superb Art Deco interior.

In a street full of *crêperies*, don't miss the magnificent **Crêperie de Josselin (126)** (€) *(67 rue du Montparnasse, 14th, 01-43.20.93.50; hours: Tu–Su 12PM–11PM)*;

lovely, romantic, and as relaxed as the Breton country-side, the whole experience is most satisfying. If you have a hankering for Italian, **Auberge de Venise (127)** (€€) *(10 rue Delambre, 14th, 01-43.35.43.09; hours: M 7PM–11:30PM, Tu–Su 12PM–2:30PM, 7PM–11:30PM)* assures exceptional food in a comfortable ambience.

In the tiny, classic bistro **Chez Marcel (128)** (€€) *(7 rue Stanislas, 6th, 01-45.48.29.94; hours: M–F 12PM–2PM, 7:30PM–10PM, closed Aug)* you feel like you're a guest in the chef's home: good Lyonnais cuisine is matched by friendly service and down-home décor. Imaginative bistro fare and a great wine list put **Wadja (129)** (€€) *(10 rue de la Grande-Chaumière, 6th, 01-46. 33.02.02; hours: M–Sa 12PM–2PM, 7:30PM–11PM)* on the "good value" list. **Caméléon (130)** (€€-€€€) *(6 rue de Chevreuse, 6th, 01-43.27.43.27; hours: Tu–Sa 12:30PM– 2PM, 7:30PM– 10PM)* is an old-fashioned bistro—homey with unpretentious classic French food.

Bars & Nightlife:

Watch the world go by at the famous café-bars on **Blvd. du Montparnasse**: La Coupole **(117)** *(No. 102, see pages 161 & 163)*, Le Dôme **(125)** *(No. 108, see page 163)*, or **Le Select (132)** *(99 bd. du Montparnasse, 6th, 01-45.48.38.24; hours: M–Th, Su 7AM–2AM, F–Sa 7AM–4AM)*. The **Fondation Cartier (124)** *(see also page 162)* hosts very hip arts soirées. **Rosebud (133)** *(11 bis,* *rue Delambre, 14th, 01-43.35.38.54; hours: 7PM–2AM),* a 1950s-style café-bar, attracts a chic, more mature (30ish to 50ish), arty and media crowd with its retro glamour.

WHERE TO SHOP

The **open-air food market** at **rue Daguerre (134)** *(between ave. du Maine and ave. du Général-Leclerc, 14th; hours: morning, late afternoon)* is a daily feast. But food isn't the only offering here: **Divine (135)** *(39 rue Daguerre, 14th, 01-43.22.28.10; hours: Tu–Sa 10:30AM–1PM, 3PM–7:30PM)* sells berets, hats, scarves, and gloves for men and women. Adorable outfits for children, linens, lace, robes, nightgowns, cosmetics, and food products, all made by nuns and monks throughout France, are sold at **La Boutique de l'Artisanat Monastique (136)** *(68 bis, ave. Denfert-Rochereau, 14th, 01-43.35.15.76)*; the quality and workmanship are beautiful.

WHERE TO STAY

An international clientele helps create an appealing atmosphere at **Hôtel Lenox Montparnasse (137)** *(€-€€) (15 rue Delambre, 14th, 01-43.35.34.50, www.hotel lenox.com)*, where personality makes up for bedroom size. Surrealist André Breton once lived in the building now occupied by **Hôtel Delambre (138)** *(€) (35 rue Delambre, 14th, 01-43.20.66.31, www.hoteldelambre. com)*, a nicely remodeled, comfortable, affordable sleep. More formal, **Hôtel l'Aiglon (139)** *(€-€€) (232 bd. Raspail, 14th, 01-43.20.82.42, www.hotel-paris-aiglon.com)* is discreet and tasteful.

r. Carpeaux
r. Lamarck
r. Duhesme
r. de la Fontaine du But
LAMARCK CAULAINC M (12)
r. Joseph de Maistre
r. Eugène
F. Zien
Damrémont
r. Caulaincourt
r. Lam
Saules
r. Paul F
r. Etex
Stienlen
r. Juste Métivier
16
St-Vincent
7
av. Junot
r. S. Dereure
r. Giraldon
r. de l'Abreuvoir
13
Corto
Cimetiere
de
Montmartre
41
r. Tourlaque
r. Lepic
9
8
17
r. Norvins
r. St-Rustique
pl. du Calvaire
12
r. Norvins
6
Gabrie
r. J. de Maistre
39
r. Tholozé
Durantin
d'Orchampt
r. de la Mire
Garreau
r. Berthe
14
39
10
24
18
r. Caulaincourt
av. Rachel
r. Cauchois
r. Lepic
r. A. P.
Bruant
des
Abbesses
19
r. R.
r. Audran
ABBESSES M (12)
r. de la Vieuville
1
20
Planquette
r. Véron
Garreau
Trois
21
PIGALLE
v. des Platanes
c. G.
Pilon
c. C. Piémontesi
r. Y. Le Tac
r. des Martyrs
2
7
55
42
r. Coustou
45
43
r. P. Haret
r. Lepic
c. C. Véron
BLANCHE M (2)
bd. de Clichy
r. de Bruxelles
c. du Midi
v. de Guelma
r. A. Antoine
Houdon
51
11
44
60
r. de Calais
r. Fontaine
r. Germain Pilon
47
48
r. du Calais
r. Mansart
Fromentin
pl. PIGALLE M (2,12)
Pigalle
59
r. Ballu
r. de Blanche
r. Duperré
Douai
av. Frochot
r. A. Stevens
Violet le Duc
r. Moncey
r. P. Escudier
r. Heinter
Chaptal
r. Frochot
Malesherbes
r. La Bruyère
r. Pigalle
r. Victor Massé
46
r. de la Rochefoucauld
r. Notre Dame de Lorette
r. H. Monnier
r. de Navarin
r. Clauzel
r. Laferrière
ST-GEORGES M (12)
r. des Martyrs
r. Manuel
r. C
0   0.25 mile
0   0.25 km
pl. d'Estienne d'Orves
r. d'Aumale
r. de Clichy
r. St-Lazare

chapter 7

MONTMARTRE

PIGALLE

Places to See:

1. Place des Abbesses
2. St-Jean-de-Montmartre
3. Chapelle du Martyre
4. Square Willette
5. SACRÉ-COEUR ★
6. Place du Tertre
7. Au Lapin Agile
8. Moulin de la Galette
9. Avenue Junot
10. Le Bateau-Lavoir
11. Max Fourny Museum of Naïf Art
12. Espace Montmartre Salvador Dali
13. Musée de Montmartre
14. Studio 28
15. Théâtre de l'Atelier
41. Montmartre Cemetery
42. Moulin Rouge
43. Museum of Eroticism

Places to Eat & Drink:

16. Le Maquis
17. Le Moulin de la Galette
18. Le Soleil Gourmand
19. Café Burq
20. La Famille
21. L'Annexe
22. L'Entracte
24. Doudingue
44. L'Homme Tranquille
45. Chez Toinette
46. Rose Bakery
47. Le Divan du Monde
48. La Fourmi

Where to Shop:

27. Gaspard de la Butte
28. Pages 50/70: Olivier Verlet
29. Zelia sur la Terre comme au Ciel
30. Galerie Christine Diegoni
33. Belle de Jour
34. Marché St-Pierre
35. SN Style
36. Luc Dognin
37. Lily Latifi
50. Et puis c'est tout
51. Emmanuelle Zysman
52. Heaven
53. Patricia Louisor
54. FuturWare Lab/Tatiana Lebedev

As an artist, a man has no home
in Europe save in Paris.

—*Friedrich Nietzsche*

MONTMARTRE

⑫ *to Abbesses or Lamarck-Caulaincourt*

• SNAPSHOT •

For centuries Montmartre was a serene village, full of windmills, thatched cottages, and vineyards. However, it gained its name by quite an un-serene history. It is the site of the beheading of St. Denis and other Christian priests by the Romans in A.D. 250. The *Mons Martyrum*, or Mound of the Martyrs, later evolved into Montmartre. The highest point in the city, it became part of Paris in 1860 but retained its village-like character, regardless of Baron Haussmann's renovations. From the 1880s artists began moving into the area, giving it the bohemian lifestyle and reputation for which it is still known today. Montmartre was the inspiration for works by Renoir, Toulouse-Lautrec, Utrillo, Modigliani, and Picasso, among others. Atop the hill the enormous basilica of Sacré-Coeur, with its pristine white dome, is visible from just about anywhere in Paris; from there the panorama of the city unfolds in all its glory. Today, Montmartre is again a quarter of emerging young artists and the next generation of fashion designers. It retains its village-like charm, and the romantic aura of the streets on the hill never seems to fade. Make sure to roam those streets to absorb the allure of the quarter and note its many beautiful details.

PLACES TO SEE
Landmarks:

Only two métro stations still have their original Art Nouveau, wrought-iron and glass-canopied entrances designed by Hector Guimard: Porte Dauphine, on Paris's western edge, and Abbesses, in the heart of Montmartre at **Place des Abbesses (1)** *(18th)*, a lively, picturesque square. **St-Jean-de-Montmartre (2)** *(19 rue des Abbesses, 18th, 01-46.06.43.96; call for hours, guided tours Sa 4:30PM)*, the first church to be built of reinforced concrete, is faced with brick; its door is inlaid with turquoise mosaics, and the interior is Art Nouveau with details borrowed from Islamic architecture. Legend has it that when St. Denis, the first bishop of Paris, was decapitated in a medieval chapel, he picked up his head and walked away. Today, the **Chapelle du Martyre (3)** *(9 rue Yvonne-le-Tac, 18th; hours: open)* stands on that site.

TOP PICK!

A short walk along rue Tardieu brings you to **Square Willette (4)** *(18th)*. With lawns, trees, shrubs, and flowerbeds terraced into its hillside setting, ★**SACRÉ-COEUR (5)** *(35 rue du Chevalier de la Barre, 18th, 01-53.41.89.00, www.sacre-coeur-montmartre.com; hours: 6AM–11PM; dome hours: summer 9AM–7PM, winter 9AM–6PM)*, the **Basilica of the Sacred Heart**, is a grand Roman-Byzantine church. During the Franco-Prussian war of 1870 and Otto von Bismarck's siege of Paris, two businessmen made a private vow to God to build a church if France was spared destruction. The building was consecrated in 1919, when a victorious France emerged from World War I, another war with Germany. To reach it, walk up the many steps, take the *funiculaire*, or wind your way up rue Ronsard, rue Maurice-Utrillo, and onto the square of the basilica, the *parvis*. The church is full of wonderful mosaics, statues, relief sculptures, and stained glass. The fabulous architecture is capped by the famous ovoid dome, the second highest point in Paris after the Eiffel Tower.

West of the basilica is the **Place du Tertre (6)** *(18th)*, full of quick-draw portraitists and swamped with tourists. Another Montmartre legend is that the term "bistro" originated here in the early 1800s when Russian soldiers in the restaurant **La Mère Catherine** shouted "Bistro!" ("Quickly!") for faster service. Northward, the cabaret **Au Lapin Agile (7)** *(22 rue des Saules, 18th, 01-46. 06.85.87, www.au-lapin-agile.com; hours: Tu–Su 9PM–2AM)* retains its early 20th-century atmosphere when it was a favorite of artists and poets. Of the old village windmills, two remain, both in rue Lepic: Moulin du Radet (further down) and **Moulin de la Galette (8)** *(rue Lepic and rue Tholoze, 18th)*, which became a dancehall that inspired work by

Vincent van Gogh and Auguste Renoir. Many painters lived and had studios in tranquil **Avenue Junot (9)** *(18th)*. Nearby on a lovely square, **Le Bateau-Lavoir (10)** *(13 pl. Emile-Goudeau, 18th; closed to public)* was a neglected, run-down building of artists' studios and apartments shared in the early 1900s by Modigliani, Picasso, Braque, Juan Gris, and Marie Laurencin, among others. Here, in 1907, Picasso painted *Les Demoiselles d'Avignon*, considered the painting that launched Cubism. Now rebuilt, this historical building again provides studio and living space for emerging artists.

Arts & Entertainment:

The **Max Fourny Museum of Naïf Art (11)** *(Halle St-Pierre, 2 rue Ronsard, 18th, 01-42.58.72.89, www.hallesaint pierre.org; hours: 10AM–6PM, Aug M–F 12PM–6PM)* contains paintings and sculptures from more than 30 countries. Near the Place du Tertre, the **Espace Montmartre Salvador Dali (12)** *(11 rue Poulbot, 18th, 01-42.64.40.10, www.daliparis.com; hours: 10AM–6PM)* exhibits the Surrealist artist's work. The **Musée de Montmartre (13)** *(12 rue Cortot, 18th, 01-46.06.61.11; hours: Tu–Su 11AM–6PM)* covers the history of Montmartre and its bohemian life, and includes a reconstruction of the Café de l'Abreuvoir, Utrillo's favorite café.

The art cinema **Studio 28 (14)** *(10 rue Tholozé, 18th, 01-46.06.36.07, www.cinemastudio28.com; call for show times or check Web site)* was decorated by Jean Cocteau. The **Théâtre de l'Atelier (15)** *(1 pl. Charles-Dullin, 18th, 01-46.06.49.24, www.theatre-atelier.com; call for show* *times or check Web site)* stages contemporary plays, both French and international.

PLACES TO EAT & DRINK
Where to Eat:

In an area that's a known tourist trap, **Le Maquis (16)** (€–€€) *(69 rue Caulaincourt, 18th, 01-42.59.76.07; hours: M–Sa 12PM–2PM, 7:45PM–10PM)* is a good neighborhood restaurant serving traditional dishes prepared with fresh, seasonal ingredients. **Le Moulin de la Galette (17)** (€€–€€€) *(83 rue Lepic, 18th, 01-46.06.84.77, www.le moulindelagalette.fr; hours: 12PM–11PM)*, by the famous windmill, is a stunning, romantic locale with delectable food. A trendy, artistic Montmartre crowd converges on **Le Soleil Gourmand (18)** (€) *(10 rue Ravignan, 18th, 01-42.51.00.50; hours: M–Su 12PM–2:30PM, 7:30PM–11PM)*: the food is simple; the ambience outstanding. Also super-hip is **Café Burq (19)** (€€) *(6 rue Burq, 18th, 01-42.52.81.27; hours: M–Sa 6PM–2AM)*, with terrific New French Bistro fare, a great atmosphere, and music to match.

A talented Basque chef with culinary inspiration from Southeast Asia, Latin America, North Africa, and France has a hit on his hands: **La Famille (20)** (€€) *(41 rue des Trois-Frères, 18th, 01-42.52.11.12; hours: Tu–Sa 8PM–11PM)* is one of the trendiest Parisian restaurants. The atmosphere is relaxed with a friendly and cool crowd, and good music to boot. Cheap, cheap, cheap: **L'Annexe (21)** (€) *(13 rue des Trois-Frères, 18th, 01-46.06.12.48, www.lannexe-montmartre.fr; hours: M–Sa 7PM–2AM)* isn't haute anything; its simple, good, inexpensive food comes in large portions. **L'Entracte (22) (€€)** *(44 rue d'Orsel, 18th, 01-46.06.93.41; hours: W–Sa 12PM–2PM, 7PM–10:30PM, Su 12PM–2PM)*, a tiny, intimate bistro, does classic French dishes very well.

Bars & Nightlife:

For songs of the good old days, the cabaret **Au Lapin Agile (7)** *(see also page 171)* has just the right touch of nostalgia. **Doudingue (24)** *(24 rue Durantin, 18th, 01-42.54.88.08; hours: M–Sa 6PM–2AM, Su 11AM–6PM)* means "crazy but nice," apt for this bar furnished with a mix of Baroque, Oriental, and flea market; DJs spin discs and there's a menu of health food.

WHERE TO SHOP

Designer children's clothes at **Gaspard de la Butte (27)** *(10 bis, rue Yvonne-le-Tac, 18th, 01-42.55.99.40, www. gasparddelabutte.com)* are beautiful, fanciful, and imaginative. Modern designs in glass, ceramics, and lighting are fabulous at **Pages 50/70: Olivier Verlet (28)** *(15 rue Yvonne-le-Tac, 18th, 01-42.52.48.59, www.pages50-70. com; hours: Tu–Sa 2PM–7:30PM, Su–M by appt)*.

Rue d'Orsel is full of wonderful boutiques, such as **Zelia sur la Terre comme au Ciel (29)** *(47 ter, rue d'Orsel, 18th, 01-46.06.96.51, www.zelia.net; by appt only)*, an extravagant, imaginative wedding shop. Look for high-design furniture and objects at **Galerie Christine Diegoni (30)** *(47 ter, rue d'Orsel, 18th, 01-42.64.69.48, www. christinediegoni.fr)*. **Belle de Jour (33)** *(7 rue Tardieu, 18th, 01-46.06.15.28, www.belle-de-jour.fr)* has every imaginable crystal perfume bottle.

Marché St-Pierre (34) *(rue Charles-Nodier, pl. St-Pierre, 18th; hours vary; usually M 2PM–6PM, Tu–Sa 10AM–6PM)* is the place to go for fabrics and trimmings; many shops offer discounted remnants. Emerging designers favor **rue des Gardes**. SN Style (35) *(6 bis, rue des Gardes, 18th, 01-42.55.11.80; women's clothing: www.sn-style.com; men's clothing: www.sylvain-nuffer. com)* showcases fabulous, not-to-be-missed new designers. Beautifully lined, bright leather bags by Luc Dognin (36) *(4 rue des Gardes, 18th, 01-44.92.32.16, www.dognin paris.com)* are the rage all over Paris. Lily Latifi (37) *(11 rue des Gardes, 18th, 01-42.23.30.86, www. lilylatifi.com; hours: Th–Sa 2PM–7PM)* meshes industrial design with applied and visual arts to create unusual fabrics that she turns into objects, clothing, and bags.

WHERE TO STAY

Exhibitions by local artists and magnificent views are some of the highlights of the formal but not pretentious Terrass Hôtel (38) (€€-€€€) *(12 rue Joseph-de-Maistre, 18th, 01-46.06.72.85, www.terrass-hotel.com)*. You get value for money at the quiet, clean, family-run Hôtel des Arts (39) (€-€€) *(5 rue Tholozé, 18th, 01-46.06.30.52, www.arts-hotel-paris.com)*. It's quite an uphill hike from the métro, but the views are spectacular at the romantic, antique-filled Ermitage Hôtel (40) (€) *(24 rue Lamarck, 18th, 01-42.64.79.22, www.ermitagesacrecoeur.fr)*.

PIGALLE

2 **12** *to Pigalle;* **2** *to Blanche or Anvers*

• SNAPSHOT •

Pigalle, once the sleazy red-light center of Paris, has begun cleaning up its neighborhood of streetwalkers, peep shows, and erotic cabarets. That cabaret scene was immortalized in the posters that Toulouse-Lautrec made of characters and places in Pigalle. His renderings of *danseuse* Jane Avril at dancehalls such as the Moulin Rouge, the Divan Japonais, and Le Chat Noir, as well as his posters of *chansonnier* Aristide Bruant added atmosphere to the seediness of the quarter renowned for its brothels.

PLACES TO SEE
Landmarks:

Famous artists and infamous characters are buried in **Montmartre Cemetery (41)** *(20 ave. Rachel, 18th, 01-53.42.36.30; hours: Mar 16–Nov 5, M–F 8AM–6PM, Sa 8:30AM–6PM, Su 9AM–6PM; Nov 6–Mar 15 M–F 8AM–5:30PM, Sa 8:30AM–5:30PM, Su 9AM–5:30PM):* dancer Nijinsky, filmmaker Truffaut, painter Degas, composers Berlioz and Offenbach, and writers Stendhal and Dumas *fils* lie beside La Goulue (Louise Weber, the first can-can performer and Toulouse-Lautrec's model), Alphonsine Plessis (consumptive inspiration for Dumas' *La Dame aux Camélias*), and famed beauty Madame de Récamier.

The **Moulin Rouge (42)** *(82 bd. de Clichy, 18th, 01-53.09.82.82, www.moulin rouge.fr; show times: 9PM, 11PM; matinees 2:45PM)* was once a baudy, populist cabaret theatre. Today, while they still do the can-can there, it holds none of the original naughty atmosphere but is instead an expensive, Las Vegas-style tourist trap.

Arts & Entertainment:

In keeping with its location among the sex shops and shows of Pigalle, the **Museum of Eroticism (43)** *(72 bd. de Clichy, 18th, 01-42.58.28.73, www.musee-erotisme.com; hours: 10AM–2AM)* focuses on sex as a motif of folk art. On display are phalluses, fertility symbols, figurines, pictures, and a history of Parisian brothels. Instructive and funny, at times seedy, it's not erotic in itself.

PLACES TO EAT & DRINK
Where to Eat:

Basic food in a funky décor (read: garage-sale furnishings) is what the family-owned **L'Homme Tranquille (44)** *(€-€€) (81 rue des Martyrs, 18th, 01-42.54.56.28; hours: 7PM–11:30PM)* offers. Locals know that **Chez Toinette (45)** *(€-€€) (20 rue Germain Pilon, 18th, 01-42.54.*

44.36; hours: Tu–Sa 8PM–11PM, book ahead) is a good deal: the young, arty clientele loves the fun, casual atmosphere and fills up on French home cooking. **Rose Bakery (46) (€)** *(46 rue des Martyrs, 9th, 01-42.82.12.80; hours: Tu–Sa 9AM–7PM, Su 10AM–5PM, closed 2 wks Aug)* has all things English but is especially good for tea and dessert.

Bars & Nightlife:

Though the **Moulin Rouge (42)** *(see also page 177)* has become a cheesy venue catering to tourists, other cabarets have turned into hip clubs. **Rue des Martyrs** is a happening spot. Toulouse-Lautrec's Le Divan Japonais has become **Le Divan du Monde (47)** *(75 rue des Martyrs, 18th, 01-42.52.02.46, www.divandumonde.com; hours vary)*, featuring a wide range of music, from hip-hop to Cuban, reggae to techno-pop, in a laid-back setting. At night the hip **La Fourmi (48)** *(74 rue des Martyrs, 18th, 01-42.64.70.35; hours: M–Th 8:30AM–2AM, F–Sa 8:30AM–4AM, Su 10AM–2AM)* attracts both party-till-dawners and casual drinkers, goths, and the flannel-shirted set.

WHERE TO SHOP

Cutting-edge design characterizes **rue des Martyrs**. Vintage French 1950s-1970s objects and furnishings make Et puis c'est tout (50) *(72 rue des Martyrs, 9th, 01-40.23.94.02; hours: M 2PM–7PM, Tu–Sa 12PM–7PM)* stand out. Inspired by 1930s music-halls, photographs, and flea markets, the stylish bags of Emmanuelle Zysman (51) *(81 rue des Martyrs, 18th, 01-42.52.01.00,* *www.emmanuellezysman.fr; hours: Tu–F 11AM–7PM, Sa 12PM–8PM, Su 3:30PM–7PM)* are sold around the world. Elegance is the by-word at Heaven (52) *(83 rue des Martyrs, 18th, 01-44.92.92.92, www.heaven-paris.com; hours: Tu–Sa 11AM–7:30PM, Su 2PM–7:30PM)*, where a fashion designer and lighting creator have teamed up to showcase their works. Simple, unique, and beautiful, Patricia Louisor (53) *(16 rue Houdon, 18th, 01-42. 62.10.42, www.patricialouisor.com; hours: 12PM–8PM* clothes are "for working, dancing, or seduction." Architectural lines in soft, luxurious fabrics give the clothes at FuturWare Lab/Tatiana Lebedev (54) *(2 rue Piémontési, 18th, 01-42.01.25.93)* a futuristic edge.

WHERE TO STAY

Paris Vacation Apartments (55) (€-€€€) *(86 bd. de Clichy, 18th, 06-09.65.94.55 or 06-12.44.64.78, www. parisvacationapartments.com)* offer studios and apartments on a weekly rental basis to make you feel at home while taking in the city sights.

FLEA MARKET OF ST-OUEN **8**

r. du Président Wilson

r. Victor Hugo

bd. Bessières

bd. Victor Hugo

bd. Berthier

17^E

LA DÉFENSE **9**

av. Charles de Gaulle

r. de

bd. des Batignolles

pl. du
Mal Juin

r. du

bd. de Courcelles

bd. des

r. de
Rome

pl. de
l'Europe

d'S

d'C

av. de la
Grande Armée

pl. des
Ternes

av. Hoche

Malsherbes

av. de Friedland

bd. Haussmann

8^E

BOIS DE
BOULOGNE **1**

av. Foch

pl. Charles
de Gaulle/
Etoile

av. de

Faubourg St-Honoré

av. des Champs-Elysées

bd. Lannes

av. Victor Hugo

av. Kléber

pl. de la
Concorde

r. de Rivo

16^E

pl. du
Trocadero

q. des Tuilerie

av. Paul Doumet

av. de la Bourdonnais

pl. des
Invalides

7^E

allée de Longchamp

av. Mozart

r. la Fontaine

r. de Grenelle

bd. Garibaldi

pl.
Vauban

r. de Babylone

bd. R

pl. Jean-
Lorrain

av. de Versailles

av. Emile Zola

r. de la Convention

r. de Sèvres

r. de Rennes

André Citroën

r. Lecourbe

r. de Vaugirard

Raspail

Montparnasse

PARC
& ANDRÉ
CITROËN **2**

r. Balard

bd. Victor

15^E

av. du Maine

Seine

bd. Périphérique

bd. Lefebvre

bd. Brune

av. du C

1

Paris Overview
Arrondissements

0   1 m
0   1 km

chapter 8

OUTSKIRTS
OF PARIS

Places to See:

1. Bois de Boulogne
2. Parc André Citroën
3. Bois de Vincennes
4. Père Lachaise Cemetery
5. Belleville/Ménilmontant
6. Parc des Buttes-Chaumont
7. Parc de la Villette: City of Science; City of Music
8. Flea Market of St-Ouen
9. La Grande Arche de la Défense

I could spend my whole life
watching the Seine flow by...
It is a poem of Paris.

—Blaise Cendrars

At the farther reaches of Paris are a number of notable spots that make for a lovely few hours or even a whole day. Although exploring these areas is recommended, it is not advisable to walk around the parks at night. These areas are at some distance from the main attractions of the city, so it is preferable to find a hotel in central Paris rather than in such outlying spots.

BOIS DE BOULOGNE (1) *(16th)*

② to Porte Dauphine; **①** to Porte Maillot or Les Sablons; **⑩** to Porte d'Auteuil

West of Paris is the **Bois de Boulogne**, a stunning park of more than 2,000 acres. Once the royal hunting grounds, it is a magical forest with gardens, woods, lakes, châteaux, and racetracks, an idyllic place for walking, boating, bicycling, and other outdoor recreation. To tour the vast grounds, rent a bicycle near **Pavillon Royal** *(rte. de Suresnes)*, a short walk from the Art Nouveau

métro station **Porte Dauphine** *(M: 2)*. Among the features of the Bois are the **Jardin d'Acclimatation** *(01-40.67.90.82, www.jardindacclimatation.fr, hours: May–Sep 10AM–7PM; Oct–Apr 10AM–6PM)*, a children's amusement park; the **Parc de Bagatelle** *(rte. de Sèvres à Neuilly)*, a park and château; and the romantic garden **Pré Catelan**, site also of a famous restaurant. The **Shakespeare Garden** contains flowers, trees, and plants that appear in the poet's plays, as well as an open-air theatre. Two lakes, **Lac Supérieur** and **Lac Inférieur**, offer boating opportunities. France's two

most famous horseracing tracks, **Hippodrome de Longchamp** *(rte. des Tribunes, 01-44.30.75.00, www. france-galop.com; call for race times or check Web site)* and **Hippodrome d'Auteuil** *(rte. d'Auteuil aux Lacs, 01-40.71.47.47, www.france-galop.com; call for race times or check Web site)*, are located in the Bois. The **Stade Roland-Garros** *(Porte des Mousquetaires, 2 ave. Gordon-Bennett, 01-47.43.48.00, or book tours at, 01.47.43.48.48, www.fft.fr/rolandgarros/fr; museum hours: Tu–Su 10AM–6PM, closed during French Open)* hosts the annual French Open Tennis Championships *(late May–early June)*. Kings kept their mistresses in châteaux in the Bois de Boulogne, giving the park its reputation for love; today, night brings out transsexuals and swingers of all sorts.

The French gastronomic treasure **Le Pré Catelan** **(€€€€)** *(rte. de Suresnes, 16th, 01-44.14.41.14, www. lenotre.fr; hours: Nov–Apr Tu–Sa 12PM–1:30PM, 7:30PM–9:30PM; May–Oct Tu–Sa 12PM–1:30PM, 7:30PM–9:30PM, Su 12PM–1:30PM)* serves exquisite French cuisine in a romantic setting. There are numerous restaurants (mostly elegant and expensive) and cafés in the park. A boat ride and enchanting outdoor setting enhance the dining experience at **Le Chalet des Iles** **(€€)**

*(on the larger island of **Lac Inférieur**, 01-42.88.04.69, www.chaletdesiles.net; hours: 12PM–2:30PM, 8PM–10:30PM).*

PARC ANDRÉ CITROËN (2) *(15th)*

8 to Balard; **10** to Javel/André-Citroën

Parc André Citroën *(Quai André-Citroën; hours: M–F 8AM–dusk, Sa–Su 9AM–dusk)*, built on the grounds of the old Citroën car factory, is a marvel of landscape architecture. Greenhouses, ponds, fountains, gardens, and inventive formations of hedges and trees blend into a wonderland of primitive and formal nature.

BOIS DE VINCENNES (3) *(12th)*

1 to Château de Vincennes;
8 to Porte de Charenton or Porte Dorée

Like the Bois de Boulogne, the **Bois de Vincennes** *(www.boisdevincennes.com)* was once a royal hunting ground. On the southeast edge of Paris, it is home to a famous zoo, a floral garden, racetrack, château and fortress, and various sports and horticultural sites. Along the north side, the **Château de Vincennes** *(entry by the Tour du Village 1, ave. de Paris, 01-48.08.31.20; hours: Apr–Sep 10AM–12PM, 1PM–6PM; Oct–Mar 10AM–12PM, 1PM–5PM)*, a medieval fortified castle, has been a royal residence, prison, porcelain factory, and arsenal. The **castle keep** is the château's museum. Nearby is **Parc Floral** *(rte. du Champ de Manoeuvre, 12th, 01-49.57.24.84, www.parcfloralde paris.com)*, a botanic garden. The three lakes—**Lac des Minimes**, **Lac Daumesnil**, and **Lac de Gravelle**—are beautiful areas for walking and boating. In the **Parc Zoologique** *(53 ave. de St-Maurice; hours: M–Su 9AM– 5:30PM)* animals roam freely within large enclosures resembling their natural habitats. The Bois also houses the **Buddhist Temple of Paris** *(rte. de la Ceinture du Lac Daumesnil, 01-40.04.98.06, www.kagyu-dzong.org; call for hours)* and the **Aquarium of Tropical Fish** *(293 ave. Daumesnil, 01-44.74.84.80, www.palais-portedoree.org; hours: W–M 10AM–5:15PM)*.

Deep within the Bois is the **Cartoucherie de Vincennes** *(rte. du Champ de Manoeuvre; from Métro Château de Vincennes, free shuttle bus, or bus 112)*; once a munitions warehouse, it became home to some of the world's best avant-garde theatre during the politically turbulent 1960s. Most famous of the five troupes housed there, the **Théâtre du Soleil** *(theatre 01-43.74.87.63, box office 01-43.74.24.08, www.theatre-du-soleil.fr)* is a must-see for anyone interested in theatre. The troupe creates grand political epics using masks, puppets, and musicians, and drawing on international theatre traditions. The other troupes are also inspiring: **Théâtre de l'Aquarium** *(01-43.74.99.61, www.theatredelaquarium.com)*; **Théâtre de la Tempête** *(01-43.28.36.36, www.la-tempete.fr)*; **Théâtre de l'Epée de Bois** *(01-48.08.39.74, www.epeedebois.com)*; and **Théâtre du Chaudron** *(01-43.28.97.04)*.

In the park there is a **café** (on **Reuilly Island** in Lac Daumesnil) and a **restaurant** (on **Porte Jaune Island** in Lac des Minimes). Theatrical productions at the **Cartoucherie** have the bonus of good food in the **lobby cafés**: the soup, bread, and sandwiches are homemade. A tiny treasure in a former butcher shop, **Les Zygomates** (€-€€) *(7 rue de Capri, 12th, 01-40. 19.93.04, www. zygomates.com; hours: Tu–Sa 12PM–2PM, 7:30PM– 10:30PM, closed Aug)* serves excellent cuisine with a flair. Great Gascon food at the homey **Au Trou Gascon** (€€€) *(40 rue Taine, 12th, 01-43.44.34.26, www.autrougas con.fr; hours: M–F 12PM–2PM, 7:30PM–10:30PM, closed Aug)* includes *foie gras* and *cassoulet*.

PÈRE LACHAISE CEMETERY (4) *(20th)*

②③ *to Père Lachaise;* **②** *to Philippe Auguste*

Paris's most famous and most prestigious cemetery, **Père Lachaise** *(16 rue du Repos, at bd. de Ménilmontant, 20th, 01-55.25.82.10, www.pere-lachaise.com or www.pariscemeteries.com; hours: Mar 16–Nov 5 M–F 8AM–6PM, Sa 8:30AM–6PM, Su 9AM–6PM; Nov 6–Mar 15 M–F 8AM–5:30PM, Sa 8:30AM–5:30PM, Su 9AM–5:30PM)*, set on a wooded hill, is full of beautiful tombstones and funerary sculptures. Famous people interred here include Proust, Delacroix, Edith Piaf, Colette, Chopin, Balzac, Sarah Bernhardt, Oscar Wilde, Simone Signoret and Yves Montand, Alfred de Musset, Molière, La Fontaine, Abélard and Héloïse, Jim Morrison, Gertrude Stein and Alice B. Toklas, Richard Wright, Isadora Duncan, and Baron Haussmann.

The décor is run down, but the food and atmosphere at **Maison d'Italie (€)** *(27 ave. Gambetta, 20th, 01-46.36.74.75; hours: M–Su 11:30AM–3PM, 6:30PM–12AM)* are delightful. The cozy, intimate West African restaurant **Waly Fay (€–€€)** *(6 rue Godefroy-Cavaignac, 11th, 01-40.24.17.79, M: 9 to Charonne; hours: M–Sa 8PM–2AM, Su 12PM–5PM)* serves perfumed spicy stews and other delicacies in an elegant, warm ambience.

The retro music bar-café **Le Piston Pélican** *(15 rue de Bagnolet, 20th, 01-43.70.35.00; hours: M–F 8AM–2AM, Sa–Su 10AM–2AM)*, with its atmospheric vintage bar and dining area resembling a train station waiting room, attracts a hip young crowd. In what was once a railway station, the trendy bar **La Flèche d'Or** (*102 bis, rue de Bagnolet, 20th, 01-44.64.01.02, www.flechedor.com; hours: Tu–F 6:30PM–2AM, Sa–Su 10AM–2AM*) gives free concerts on weeknights (*6PM*).

BELLEVILLE/MÉNILMONTANT (5) (*20th*)

❷ ⓫ *to Belleville;* **❷** *to Couronnes or Ménilmontant;* **⓫** *to Pyrénées or Jourdain*

Belleville and **Ménilmontant**, the hilly area between Père Lachaise Cemetery and the Parc des Buttes-Chaumont, has seen a succession of some 60 different immigrant populations over the years, giving it a lively, diverse character. Edith Piaf, the torch singer who rose from poverty to international fame, was born at 72 rue de Belleville. Piaf memorabilia are gathered at the **Edith Piaf Museum** (*5 rue Crespin-du-Gast, 11th, 01-43.55.52.72; hours: by appt. only M–W 1PM–6PM*). Another famous neighborhood figure was singer and film star Maurice Chevalier. With artists and young Parisians increasingly claiming the turf, this fascinating quarter has gentrified significantly. Artists—painters, photographers, jewelers, musicians—open their studios to the public every year in mid-May at the **Portes Ouvertes** event, sponsored by the **AAB (Ateliers d'Artistes de Belleville)** (*pick up studio maps at 32 rue de la Mare, 20th, 01-46.36.44.09, www.ateliers-artistes-belleville.org, hours: gallery M–F 4PM–8PM, Sa–Su 10AM–8PM; Portes Ouvertes artists' studios 2PM–9PM*). There are lots of funky bistros, cafés, and shops in the area.

A blast from the past, **Le Bistrot des Soupirs (€-€€)** *(49 rue de la Chine, 20th, 01-44.62.93.31; hours: Tu–Sa 12PM–2:30PM, 7:30PM–10PM)* hasn't changed since the 1950s; the bistro fare and wines are classic. Refined contemporary bistro cuisine, art-deco setting, and an animated ambience is what you get at **Le Zéphyr (€€)** *(1 rue Jourdain, 20th, 01-46.36.65.81, www.lezephyrcafe.com; hours: 10AM–2AM)*. The wine bar **Le Baratin (€-€€)** *(3 rue Jouye-Rouve, 20th, 01-43.49.39.70; hours: Tu–F 12PM–1AM, Sa 6PM–1AM, closed 3 wks Aug)* serves generous portions of hearty food along with unusual wines. For great Thai, don't miss **Lao Siam (€-€€)** *(49 rue de Belleville, 19th, 01-40.40.09.68; hours: 12PM–3PM, 7PM–11:30PM)*.

Alternative cool and streetwise urban chic reigns among young designers of **rue Oberkampf**, where the bar scene buzzes at night. It all started with **Café Charbon** *(109 rue Oberkampf, 11th, 01-43.57.55.13; hours: Su–W 9AM–2AM, Th–Sa 9AM–4AM)*, the cool and stylish Belle-Époque music bar-café, and its nightclub annex **Nouveau Casino** *(01-43.57.57.40, www.nouveaucasino. net; hours: Su–W 9AM–2AM, Th–Sa 9AM–4AM)*. Celebrities and locals love the trendy, arty bar **La Mère Lachaise** *(78 bd. de Ménilmontant, 20th, 01-47.97. 61.60; hours: 9AM–2AM)*, with its fabulous terrace.

PARC DES BUTTES-CHAUMONT (6) *(19th)*

7 *to Louis Blanc, then*
7 *to Buttes Chaumont or Botzaris*

Baron Haussmann converted a garbage dump and quarry on a hill into the **Parc des Buttes-Chaumont** *(rue Manin, main entrance at rue Armand Carrel, 01-40.71.76.07; hours: summer 7:30AM–11PM, winter 7:30AM–9PM),* located in a working-class neighborhood. A lake was created, with an island and footbridge, streams, a waterfall, and beaches. A Romanesque temple stands on the hilltop.

Located within the park, **Chez Vincent Cozzoli–Pavillon Puebla (€€-€€€)** *(Parc des Buttes-Chaumont, 19th; use park entrance at 3 ave. Simon-Bolivar, 01.42.02.22.45; hours: M–Sa 7:30PM–2AM or 3AM or 'til last customer)* may be one of the best Italian restaurants in Paris. American chef Mark Singer prepares fabulously imaginative new bistro fare at his restaurant **La Cave Gourmande (€€)** *(10 rue du Général-Brunet, 19th, 01-40.40.03.30; hours: M–F 12PM–2PM, 7PM–11PM).*

PARC DE LA VILLETTE: CITY OF SCIENCE; CITY OF MUSIC (7) *(19th)*

7 *to Porte de la Villette;* **5** *to Porte de Pantin*

Built on what was once the city's slaughterhouses and livestock market, the sprawling **Parc de la Villette** is home to an amazing complex of museums and exhibition halls. The **Cité des Sciences et de l'Industrie** *(30 ave. Corentin-Cariou, 19th, 01-40.05.70.00, www.cite-sciences.fr; hours: Tu–Sa 10AM–6PM, Su 10AM–7PM)* reveals the world of science and technology through multimedia exhibits, interactive displays, films, and conferences. The smaller **Cité de la Musique** *(221 ave. Jean-Jaurès, 19th, 01-44.84.44.84, www.cite-musique.fr; hours: Tu–Sa 12PM–6PM, Su 1PM–6PM; Music Museum: Tu–Sa 12PM–6PM, Su 10AM–6PM)* houses, among other things, a music conservatory and a museum of music.

Head to **Avenue Jean-Jaurès** for meals or drinks. True to the district's old slaughterhouse renown, **Au Boeuf Couronné** **(€€–€€€)** *(188 ave. Jean-Jaurès, 19th, 01-42.39.44.44, www.rest-gj.com; hours: 12PM–3PM, 7PM–12AM)* serves great classic beef dishes. In turn-of-the-century décor, **Dagorno** **(€€)** *(190 ave. Jean-Jaurès, 19th, 01-40.40.09.39; call for hours)* serves wonderful traditional cuisine. **Café de la Musique** **(€€)** *(213 ave. Jean-Jaurès, 19th, 01-48.03.15.91; hours: Tu–Sa 8AM–2AM, Su–M 8AM–1AM)* is a trendy café better for people-watching than meals.

FLEA MARKET OF ST-OUEN (8) *(18th)*

4 *to Porte de Clignancourt*

Extending across 15 acres, at the largest of Parisian flea markets, the **Marché aux Puces de St-Ouen** *(main artery: rue des Rosiers, St-Ouen, just north of the 18th, Sa–M 9AM–6PM)*, some 2,500 dealers sell antiques, artwork, furniture, books, jewelry, and odds and ends. The chic, cozy brasserie **Le Soleil (€€)** *(109 ave. Michelet, St-Ouen, 01-40.10.08.08, www.restaurantlesoleil.com; hours: M–Su 12PM–3:30/4PM)* is a find in an area bereft of good restaurants.

LA GRANDE ARCHE DE LA DÉFENSE (9)
(NW border of Paris)

1 *to La Défense/Grande Arche,*
Ⓐ *to La Défense/Grande Arche*

In 1981 President François Mitterand began a campaign to construct buildings with a cultural focus. Among the many creations that resulted from this project of "Grands Travaux," or "Great Works," some of the most spectacular are the Institute of the Arab World *(see Chapter 5, page 115)*, I.M. Pei's Louvre Pyramid *(see Chapter 2, page 50)*, the Opéra Bastille *(see Chapter 4, page 97)*, and the Grande Arche of La Défense.

La Défense is a large office building complex just beyond the northwestern edge of Paris. Built in the 1960s, its skyscrapers seemed to catapult French business into the supermodern era. Here, some of Europe's tallest buildings are the workplace of more than 100,000 people. Individually, the skyscrapers are unimpressive; but taken as a whole, the development rivals business complexes in the U.S. and Asia. Into this expanse of mushrooming towers, a landmark was built in 1989 for the bicentennial of the French Revolution: the **Grande Arche** *(Paris La Défense, 01-49.07.27.27, www.grandearche.com; hours: Apr–Sep 10AM–8PM; Oct–Mar 10AM–7PM)*. It is an enormous hollow cube under which the entire cathedral of Notre Dame could fit. Inside, there is an exhibition gallery and conference center; glass elevators whisk you heavenward to the roof for a spectacular view of Paris.

chapter 9

SHORT EXCURSIONS
OUTSIDE PARIS

Places to See:
1. Versailles
2. Chartres
3. Giverny
4. Fontainebleau
5. Malmaison
6. Chantilly
7. Reims
8. Disneyland Paris
9. Parc Astérix

When I go out into the
countryside and see the sun and
the green and everything flowering,
I say to myself, "Yes indeed,
all that belongs to me!"

—*Henri Rousseau*

SHORT EXCURSIONS OUTSIDE PARIS

These areas of historic significance, cultural interest, and natural beauty can each be seen in a day trip. All have hotels for those preferring overnight stays.

VERSAILLES (1)

RER: *C5 to Versailles Rive-Gauche/Château de Versailles*
Or SNCF Train: *Gare St-Lazare station to Versailles Rive-Droite; Gare Montparnasse station to Versailles-Chantiers (average travel time: 30-45 minutes)*

Louis XIV, the "Sun King," made the palace of **Versailles** *(advance tickets at FNAC ticket offices and other outlets, see www.chateauversailles.fr; hours: Nov–Mar Tu–Su, chateau 9AM–5:30PM, estate 12PM–5:30PM, gardens 8AM–6PM; Apr–Oct Tu–Su, chateau 9AM–6:30PM, estate 12PM–7PM, gardens 7AM–7PM)* into the symbol of absolute monarchy. It remained the seat of royal political power from 1682 until the Revolution, a century later. The resplendent château, the largest in Europe, lodged 20,000 people at a time. Ornate and luxurious, it is surrounded by formal gardens with statues, canals, pools, and fountains. Louis XIV held extravagant parties and receptions here. He built a smaller palace, the **Grand Trianon**, for himself and his mistress. Later, Louis XV built the **Petit Trianon**, his own retreat, which became Marie-Antoinette's favorite.

A good seafood restaurant is **La Marée de Versailles (€€)** *(22 rue au Pain, Versailles, 01-30.21.73.73, www.restaurantlamaree.com; hours: Tu–Sa 12PM–2:15PM, 7:15PM–10:15PM)*. Tiny, quaint **Le Potager du Roy (€€-€€€)** *(1 rue du Maréchal-Joffre, Versailles, 01-39.50.35.34, www.potager-du-roi.fr; hours: Tu–Sa 12PM–1:30PM, 7:30PM–9:30PM)* serves traditional French food. Exquisite haute cuisine in an elegant ambience is a near-regal experience at **Gordon Ramsay au Trianon (€€€€)** *(Hôtel Trianon Palace, 1 bd. de la Reine, Versailles, 01-39.50.13.21; hours: Tu–Sa 11:30AM–10:30PM)*. For more info, restaurants, and accommodations, contact the **Versailles Tourist Office** *(Sofitel Building, 2 bis, ave. de Paris, 01-39.24.88.88, www.versailles-tourisme.com; hours: Apr–Sept M 10AM–6PM, Tu–Su 9AM–7PM; Oct–Mar Su–M 11AM–5PM, Tu–Sa 9AM–6PM)*.

CHARTRES (2)

SNCF Train: *Gare Montparnasse station to Chartres (average travel time: 1 hour)*

The magnificent Gothic cathedral of **Chartres** *(cathedral 02-37.21.59.08, museum 02-37.21.22.07, www.monum.fr; hours: cathedral 8:30AM–7:30PM; museum May–Aug M–Sa 9:30AM–12:30PM, 2PM–6PM; Sept–Apr M–Sa 9:30AM–12:30PM, 2PM–5PM)* is noted for its incredible stained-glass windows and its elaborately sculpted statues and reliefs. Behind the cathedral, the **Musée des Beaux-Arts** *(29 cloître Notre-Dame, 02-37.90.45.80, www.ville-chartres.fr; hours: May–Oct M, W–Sa 10AM–12PM, 2PM–6PM, Su 2PM–6PM; Nov–Apr M, W–Sa 10AM–12PM, 2PM–5PM, Su 2PM–5PM)* holds Renaissance paintings and tapestries. The **Maison de l'Archéologie** *(16 rue St-Pierre or 1 rue de l'Etroit Degré, 02-37.30.99.38, www.ville-chartres.fr or www.chartres.com; hours: July–Sept W–M 2PM–6PM; Oct–May W, Su 2PM–5PM)* recounts the story of the excavation of a Gallo-Roman city. A path along the banks of the Eure River leads to the ruins of the old Roman city wall.

There are plenty of restaurants in town; **L'Estocade** **(€-€€)** *(1 rue de la Porte-Guillaume, 02-37.34.27.17; hours: Tu–Su 12PM–2PM, 7:30PM–10PM)* has a river view. For accommodations and other info, go to the **Chartres Tourist Office** *(pl. Cathédrale, 02-37.18.26.26, www.chartres-tourisme.com; hours: Apr–Sept M–Sa 9AM–7PM, Su 9:30AM–5:30PM; Oct–Mar M–Sa 9AM–6PM, Su 9:30AM–5PM).*

GIVERNY (3)

SNCF Train: *Gare St-Lazare station to Vernon, then 3-mile taxi ride or bus (average travel time: 1 hour)*

Claude Monet lived in **Giverny** with his mistress and eight children and created his superb Impressionist paintings there. The famous water-lily pond, with its weeping willows and Japanese bridge, is a favorite spot. The house-museum, **Fondation Claude Monet** *(84 rue de Claude Monet, 02-32.51.28.21, www.fondation-monet. com; hours: Apr–Oct Tu–Su 9:30AM–6PM, come early)*, has no original Monets but plenty of memorabilia. Nearby, the **Musée Américain de Giverny** *(99 rue Claude Monet, 02-32.51.94.65, www.maag.org; hours: Apr–Oct Tu–Su 10AM–6PM)* is dedicated to American Impressionists who worked in France in Monet's time.

The famous **Hôtel Baudy (€)** *(81 rue Claude-Monet, 02-32.21.10.03; hours: Apr–Oct Tu–Sa 10AM–9:30PM, Su 10AM–2:30PM, reserve ahead)* is a museum-restaurant where some of Monet's American followers lived and worked. For overnight stays, **La Musardiere (€)** *(123 rue Claude Monet, 02-32.21.03.18, www.lamusardiere.fr)* is a lovely hotel dating back to 1880. It also features a restaurant with a terrace and garden. **Le Coin des Artistes (€)** *(65 rue Claude-Monet, 02-32.21.36.77)* is a B&B with an art gallery. For more info on Giverny, restaurants, and lodgings, go to *http://giverny.org*, or try the **Giverny Tourist Office** *(02-32.51.39.60, www.giverny-village.fr; call for hours)*.

FONTAINEBLEAU (4)

SNCF Train: *Gare de Lyon station to Fontainebleau-Avon, then bus AB, marked "Château" (buy a "Forfait Château de Fontainebleau" ticket, which includes train and bus fare, château entrance fee, and audio guide) (average travel time: 1 hour)*

Though not as sprawling or magnificent as Versailles, the **Château de Fontainebleau** *(01-60.71.50.70, www. musee-chateau-fontainebleau.fr; hours: Apr–Sept W–M 9:30AM–6PM; Oct–Mar W–M 9:30AM–5PM)*, residence of French rulers, underwent transformations that give it a mix of styles. Napoleon I built an ornate throne room and his own extravagant quarters in the palace. Explore the wonderful gardens and forest.

Rue Grande is dotted with restaurants. Try the creative cuisine at **Au Délice Impérial** *(€-€€) (1 rue Grande, 01-64.22.20.70)*. Heavy oak tables and tapestries give classic meals at **Le Caveau des Ducs** *(€-€€) (24 rue de Ferrare, 01-64.22.05.05, www.caveaudesducs.com; hours: 12PM–2PM, 7PM–10:30PM)* a 17th-century country flavor. **Hôtel Aigle Noir** *(€€) (27 pl. Napoléon-Bonaparte, 01-60.74. 60.00, www.hotelaiglenoir.fr)*, built in the 15th century, sits across from the Fontainebleau castle gardens. You'll feel at home in its warm, elegant rooms. Elegant **Hôtel Napoléon** *(€€) (9 rue Grande, 01-60.39.50.50, www. hotelnapoleon-fontainebleau.com)* is footsteps away from the château and provides a refined and charming setting. For info and maps, as well as bike rentals, go to the **Fontainebleau Area Tourist Office** *(4 rue Royale, 01-*

60.74.99.99, www.fontainebleau-tourisme.com; hours: M–Sa 10AM–6PM; Su Mar–Oct 10AM–1PM, 2PM–5:30PM, Su Nov–Mar 10AM–1PM).

MALMAISON (5)

RER: *A1 to La Défense, then bus 258 (travel time varies depending on your starting point in Paris)*

Napoleon and Josephine's love-nest **Malmaison** (*ave. du Château, 92500 Rueil-Malmaison, 01-41.29.05.55, www.chateau-malmaison.fr or www.napoleon.org; hours: Apr–Sept M, W–F 10AM–12:30PM, 1:30PM–5:45PM, Sa–Su 10AM–12:30PM, 1:30PM–6:15PM; Oct–Mar M, W–F 10AM–12:30PM, 1:30PM–5:15PM, Sa–Su 10AM–12:30PM, 1:30PM–5:45PM*) became her home after the divorce. The museum is dedicated to Napoleon and the First Empire. Don't miss Josephine's famous rose garden.

CHANTILLY (6)

SNCF Train: *Gare du Nord station to Chantilly-Gouvieux (average travel time: 30 minutes on train, plus 5-minute walk to town, 20-minute walk to château)*

Chantilly, domain of the Condé Princes, is known for its lace, for the invention of Chantilly whipped cream, and for its equestrian history of prestigious horseraces and hunting forests. The fairy tale **castle of Chantilly**, with its parks and incredible stables, houses the **Condé Museum** *(03-44.27.31.80, www.chateaudechantilly.com; hours: late Mar–early Nov W–M 10AM–6PM)*, with works by Raphael, Botticelli, Giotto, and Holbein. The **Musée Vivant du Cheval** *(Les Grandes Écuries, 03-44.27.31.80 or 03-44.57.13.13, www.museevivantducheval.fr; hours: Nov–Mar M, W–F 1PM–5PM, Sa–Su 10:30AM–5:30PM; Mar–Oct M, W–F 10:30AM–5:30PM, Sa–Su 10:30AM–6PM, open Tu as well in May–Jun)*, in the Grandes Écuries stables, shows horses and gives riding displays (first Sunday of every month). Every June, high society descends on the Chantilly racecourse for the flat-racing trophies, a prestigious and fashionable event.

The tea room in the hamlet of the castle, **Aux Goûters Champêtres (€-€€)** *(03-44.57.46.21; call for hours)*, features the famous whipped cream. On Chantilly's main street, the cozy bistro **Le Goutillon (€)** *(61 rue du Connétable, 03-44. 58.01.00)* offers home-style cooking. For info, restaurants, and lodgings, contact the **Chantilly Tourist Office** *(60 ave. Maréchal-Joffre, 03-44.67.37.37, www.chantilly-tourisme.com; hours: M–Sa 9:30AM–12:30PM, 1:30PM–5:30PM, Su May–Aug only 10AM–1:30PM)*, near the station.

REIMS (7)

SNCF Train: *Gare de l'Est station to Reims (average travel time: 90 minutes)*

Most French monarchs were crowned in Reims. **Notre-Dame de Reims** *(3 rue Guillaume de Machault, 03-26.47.55.34, www.cathedrale-reims.com; hours: 7:30AM–7:30PM)* is an ornately decorated Gothic cathedral with many beautiful stained-glass windows, including some of Chagall's designs. Located

in the region of Champagne, the area is home to France's finest bubbly. Visits to champagne houses are by appointment only: **Pommery** *(5 pl. du Général Gouraud, 03-26.61.62.55, www.pommery.com; hours: Apr–mid-Nov 9:30AM–7PM; mid-Nov–Mar 10AM–6PM)*, **Krug** *(5 rue Coquebert, 03-26.84.44.20, www.krug.com)*, **Veuve Clicquot** *(1 pl. des Droits-de-l'Homme, 03-26.89.53.90, www.veuve-clicquot.com; hours: by appt only Apr–Oct M–Sa, Nov–Mar M–F)*, **Lanson** *(66 rue de Courlancy, www.lanson.com; hours: by appt only M–F 9AM–11AM, 2PM–4PM, closed Aug)*, and **Roederer** *(21 bd. Lundy, 03-26.40.42.11, www.champagne-roederer.com; hours: by appt and recommendation)*. At **Épernay** *(18 miles away)*, **Moët et Chandon** *(20 ave. de Champagne, Épernay, 03-26.51.20.00, www.moet.com; tour hours: mid-Mar–mid-Nov M–Su 9:30AM–11:30AM, 2PM–4:30PM; mid-Nov–early Jan & early Feb–mid Mar M–F 9:30AM–11:30AM, 2PM–4:30PM; shop hours; Apr–mid-Nov 9:30AM–5:30PM, mid-Nov–Mar 9:30AM–1PM,*

2PM–5:30PM) and **Mercier** *(68 ave. de Champagne, Épernay, 03-26.51.22.22, www.champagnemercier.fr; hours: mid-Mar–mid-Nov daily 9:30AM–11:30AM, 2PM–4:30PM; mid-Feb–mid-Mar & mid-Nov–mid-Dec Th–M 9:30AM–11:30AM, 2PM–4:30PM, appts necessary only for groups of 10 or more)* do great tours.

You can find many cafés and brasseries on **Place Drouet d'Erlon** that serve good meals. Try **Aux Coteaux (€)** *(86-88 pl. Drouet d'Erlon, 03-26.47.38.84; hours: Tu–Sa 11:30AM–2PM, 6:30PM–11:45PM)* for tasty pizza and other delicious dishes. For overnight stays, Ariston Fils Champagne (€) *(4-8 Grande Rue, Brouillet, 03-26.97.43.46, book.bestwestern.com)* offers rooms in working champagne vineyards. For more info, contact the **Reims Tourist Office** *(2 rue Guillaume de Machault, 08-92.70.13.51, www.reims-tourisme.com; hours: Jan–Apr M–Sa 9AM–6PM, Su 11AM–4PM May–mid-Oct M–Sa 9AM–7PM, Su 10AM–6PM)*. In the town of **Épernay, La Cave à Champagne (€)** *(16 rue Gambetta, Épernay, 03-26.55.50.70, www.la-cave-a-champagne.com; hours: Th–M 12PM–2PM, 7PM–10PM)* is a good classic bistro. And if you get full from your meal, and fancy an overnight stay, the Hôtel de Champagne (€) *(30 rue Eugène-Mercier, Épernay, 03-26.53.10.60, book.best western.com)* is a comfortable hotel chain.

THEME PARKS:
MICKEY AND ASTÉRIX

DISNEYLAND PARIS (8)
RER: *A4 to Marne-la-Vallée/Chessy.*
(One-day RER + Disneyland Paris tickets
sold at major metro stations.)

Disneyland Paris *(Marne-la-Vallée, 08-25.30.60.30,*
www.disneylandparis.com; hours: mid-July–Aug 9AM–
11PM; Sept–mid-July M–F 10AM–8PM, Sa–Su 9AM–
8PM,) has all the usual Disney fun.

PARC ASTÉRIX (9)
RER: *B3 to Roissy/Aéroport Charles-de-Gaulle 1,*
then shuttle bus (platform A3)

At **Parc Astérix** *(60128 Plailly, 08-26.30.10.40, www.*
parcasterix.fr; hours: Apr 5–Aug 31 daily 10AM–6PM; Sept
6–Oct 26 Sa–Su 10AM–6PM; Oct 27–Nov 5 daily
10AM–6PM) the Gauls compete with Disney.

INDEX

210

211

Village Joue Club
3/5 Boulevard des
          Italiens
(m)(8) Richelien Druot
    → Creteil

Arch de Triomphe
(m)(1)(2)(6)
    Charles de Galle —
          Etoile
Sortie # 1, Champs-
Elysées / Arc de Triomphe
  signs).

Richelien Druot (m)(9)→ Pont de
  Sevres to Franklin Roosevelt,
then (m)(1) → La defense to
  Charles de Gaulle Etoile)

NOTES

NOTES

PHOTO CREDITS

Cover: © Will & Deni McIntyre/ The Image Bank

Chapters 1, 2, 4, 5, 6, 8: © Heather Zschock

Chapter 3: © Royalty-Free/Corbis

Chapter 7: © Royalty-Free/Corbis

Chapter 9: © Royalty-Free/Corbis

métro &
RER map

RAILWAY (RER)